The Upside of Digital for the Middle East and North Africa

How Digital Technology Adoption Can Accelerate Growth and Create Jobs

Ana Paula Cusolito, Clément Gévaudan,
Daniel Lederman, and Christina A. Wood

WORLD BANK GROUP

Contents

Acknowledgments . . . . *vii*

About the Authors . . . . *ix*

Executive Summary . . . . *xi*

Abbreviations . . . . *xv*

1 Introduction **1**
      References 3

**2 The Digital Paradox in the Middle East and North Africa and the
      Upside of Digital Technologies** **5**
      Notes 7
      References 7

3 Framework for Understanding the Upside of the Digital Economy **9**
      References 11

4 How Digital Technologies Help to Overcome Market Frictions **13**
      Overcoming Frictions due to Information Asymmetries on Ride-Hailing Platforms 13
      Overcoming Transport Frictions: IT Sector and Mobility Barriers in West Bank 14
      Tourism Demand: Overcoming Frictions Associated with Geography and
            Language Barriers 16
      Notes 17
      References 17

5 The Upside of Digital: Empirical Framework and Results **19**
      Lower-Bound Estimates of the Upside of the Digital Economy 19
      Gains in GDP per Capita 22
      Gains in Revenue Productivity and Employment in Manufacturing 23

Gains in Tourism and Hospitality Industry Jobs 27
Reductions in Unemployment and Increases in Female Labor Force Participation 29
Summary of the Upside Impact of Digital Technologies 32
Notes 32
References 33

6 **Three Foundational Pillars of the Digital Economy** **35**
Digital Infrastructure 35
Digital Payments 36
Regulations for E-commerce 36
Notes 38
References 38

7 **Addressing Challenges and Mitigating Risks** **39**
Liberalization and Competition as Drivers of Mobile Digital Data Technology Adoption . . 39
Competition in the Digital Services Market 41
Risk Associated with Digital Social Media 43
Data Governance 44
Data Privacy in Managing the COVID-19 Pandemic 47
Notes 48
References 48

8 **Summary and Conclusions** **51**

Appendix A: Modeling the Relationship between Digital Payments,
Bank Regulation, and Banking System Development **55**

Appendix B: Benchmark Regressions: Graphs and Statistics **59**

Appendix C: Description of New Mobile Data Technology Adoption Rankings **73**

Boxes

5.1   Empirical Framework for Estimating the Upside of Digital Technologies 20
7.1   Four Main Data Governance Paradigms 46

Figures

2.1   Penetration of Facebook Accounts and Use of Digital Payments, by Region 6
2.2   Correlation between Transparency, Trust, and Use of Digital Payments Worldwide . . . 7
3.1   Framework for Understanding the Interactions between the Development of Digital
       Infrastructure, Use of Digital Tools, and Societal Trust in Government 10
4.1   Share of Drivers Working Each Week in the Arab Republic of Egypt,
       by Driver Quality, 2018 14
4.2   Volume of Orders for Courier or Delivery Services in Jakarta, Indonesia,
       by Gender of the Driver, 2020 14
4.3   Change in Demand for Tourism Services, by Determinant 16
5.1   Simulated Schedules for Diffusion of Digital Technology, 2017–50: Linear,
       Concave, and Logit Functions 21
5.2   The Upside of Digital: Cumulative Gains in GDP per Capita in the Middle East
       and North Africa and in Sub-Saharan Africa, 2017–45 22

5.3   Digital Adoption and Export Complementarities: The Issue of Targeting 24

5.4   Cumulative Gains in Revenue Productivity in Formal Manufacturing Enterprises
        in the Middle East and North Africa and in Sub-Saharan Africa, with Perfect
        Targeting and with No Targeting. 25

5.5   Employment Gains from Website Adoption in the Middle East and North Africa
        and in Sub-Saharan Africa, with Perfect Targeting and with No Targeting 27

5.6   Estimated Gains in Tourist Arrivals due to the Adoption of B2C Tools in
        the Middle East and North Africa and in Sub-Saharan Africa, 2017–47 28

5.7   Estimated Gains in Tourism-Related Employment due to B2C Digital
        Technology Adoption in the Middle East and North Africa and in
        Sub-Saharan Africa, 2017–47 29

5.8   Decline in Unemployment due to the Diffusion of Digital Payments in the
        Middle East and North Africa and in Sub-Saharan Africa, 2017–33 30

5.9   Correlation between Digital Payments and Female Labor Force Participation, 2017 . . 31

5.10   Potential Increase in Female Labor Force Participation Rates from the
        Diffusion of Digital Payments in the Middle East and North Africa and in
        Sub-Saharan Africa, 2017–49 31

6.1   Benchmarking the Regulatory Framework for E-commerce, by Country
        Income Level. 37

7.1   Mobile Technology Adoption Rankings in the Middle East and
        North Africa and in Sub-Saharan Africa, 1981–2019. 40

7.2   ICT Regulatory Authority Independence Index in the Middle East and
        North Africa and in Sub-Saharan Africa and by Country Income Group, 2017 41

7.3   Share of Liberalized Countries in the Middle East and North Africa
        and in Sub-Saharan Africa, 2000–18. 41

7.4   Share of Foreign Participation in the Middle East and North Africa
        and in Sub-Saharan Africa, 2000–18. 42

B.1   Coverage of Information and Communication Technology Infrastructure
        in the Middle East and North Africa and Rest of the World, by
        GDP per Capita, 2019 60

B.2   Facebook and Internet Use in the Middle East and North Africa and
        Rest of the World, by GDP per Capita 62

B.3   Digital Payments and Online Purchases in the Middle East and North Africa
        and Rest of the World, by GDP per Capita 63

B.4   Use of Financial Accounts in the Middle East and North Africa and
        Rest of the World, by GDP per Capita, 2017. 64

B.5   Download Speeds in the Middle East and North Africa and
        Rest of the World, by GDP per Capita, 2019. 65

B.6   User Prices of Data in the Middle East and North Africa and
        Rest of the World, by GDP per Capita, 2019. 66

C.1   Mobile Technology Adoption Rankings in the Middle East and North Africa
        and in Sub-Saharan Africa, 1981–2019. 74

C.2   ICT Regulatory Authority Independence Index in the Middle East and
        North Africa and in Sub-Saharan Africa and by Country Income Group, 2017 75

C.3   Share of Liberalized Countries in the Middle East and North Africa
        and in Sub-Saharan Africa, 2000–18. 75

C.4   Share of Foreign Participation in the Middle East and North Africa
        and in Sub-Saharan Africa, 2000–18. 76

Tables

4.1 Change in Industry Shares of GDP in the Presence of Mobility Restrictions in West Bank, 1995–2017 15

4.2 Simulated Change in GDP in the Presence of Mobility Restrictions 15

7.1 Technology Adoption, Liberalization, and Regulatory Independence 42

7.2 Data Stewardship in a Data Governance Framework 45

7.3 Regulation on Data Privacy in the Middle East and North Africa 47

A.1 Relationships between Banking Restrictions, Financial Development, and Digital Payments 56

A.2 Description of Variables 57

B.1 ICT Infrastructure Coverage 67

B.2 ICT Adoption—Digital Finance 68

B.3 ICT Adoption—Enterprises and E-commerce 69

B.4 ICT Enablers—E-Government Development Index Subindexes 70

B.5 ICT Enablers—Quality of Institutions 71

Acknowledgments

The Middle East and North Africa (MENA) Digital Flagship is a product of the Office of the Chief Economist of the MENA Region (MNACE) of the World Bank. The report was initiated under the leadership of Rabah Arezki (former chief economist for the MENA Region) and completed under the overall guidance of Roberta Gatti (current chief economist for the MENA Region). Ana Paula Cusolito, Clément Gévaudan, Daniel Lederman, and Christina A. Wood coauthored the report.

Background research papers commissioned under the flagship program were received from Clément Gévaudan and Daniel Lederman ("Stages of Development of Payment Systems: Leapfrogging across Countries and MENA's Place in the World"); Daniel Lederman and Marwane Zouaidi ("The Digital Economy and Unemployment"); Lillyana Daza Jaller and Martin Molinuevo ("Digital Trade in MENA: Regulatory Readiness Assessment"); Mariana Viollaz and Hernan Winkler ("Does the Internet Reduce Gender Gaps? The Case of Jordan"); Nelly El-Mallakh ("Internet Job Search, Employment, and Wage Growth: Evidence from Egypt"); Ernesto Lopez-Cordova ("Digital Platforms and the Demand for Tourism Services"); Chiara Fratto and Elisa Giannone ("Market Access and Development of the ICT Sector in the West Bank"); Rabah Arezki, Vianney Dequiedt, Rachel Yuting Fan, and Carlo Maria Rossotto ("Liberalization, Technology Adoption, and Stock Returns: Evidence from Telecom"); and Ana Paula Cusolito, Daniel Lederman, and Jorge Pena ("The Effects of Digital-Technology Adoption on Productivity and Factor Demand: Firm-Level Evidence from Developing Countries"). The team thanks François de Soyres and Mohamed Abdel Jelil for their work in conceptualizing and leading the flagship program through the concept review and initiation of the research work.

The team is grateful for additional inputs received from Andrea Barone, Robert Cull, Yaroslav Eferin, Rachel Yuting Fan, Jingyu Gao, Mohamed Abdel Jelil, Davide Mare, Harish Natarajan, Carlo Maria Rossotto, and Nishta Singh. The team is also grateful for the data and graphs received from Careem (Arab Republic of Egypt) and Gojek (Indonesia) ride-hailing and package delivery companies.

Helpful guidance and comments were provided by Rabah Arezki (former MENA chief economist), Ferid Belhaj (regional vice president), Robert Cull, Mark Andrew Dutz, Lesly Goh, Michel Rogy, and François de Soyres. The team thanks discussants and other participants at a workshop held in July 2019 in Washington, DC, for their valuable feedback on early versions of the background research papers. For their constructive feedback on the preliminary findings of the report, the team also thanks participants at the seminar hosted by the Central Bank of Tunisia in November 2019, at the MNACE seminar held in March 2020, and at the meeting of the deputy finance ministers of the Arab Monetary Fund in January 2021.

The team thanks Elizabeth Forsyth for editing the manuscript and Steve Pazdan for coordinating its publication. Help from the Translation and Printing and Multimedia Units of the World Bank's Global Corporate Solutions is acknowledged. Administrative support was provided by Heran Getachew Negatu and Swati Raychaudhuri.

This flagship was completed under the strategic guidance of Ferid Belhaj.

About the Authors

Ana Paula Cusolito is a senior economist working in the Finance, Competitiveness, and Innovation Global Practice of the World Bank Group. Her research focuses on firm-level productivity, the digital economy, technology adoption, innovation, entrepreneurship, and trade. She has been involved in several recent experiments to evaluate firm-level programs aimed at increasing productivity, revamping firm demand during the COVID-19 pandemic, improving access to finance, and facilitating access to markets for small and medium enterprises. During her career, she has conducted analytical work on firm-level productivity, digital technology adoption, innovation and entrepreneurship, and international trade. She is coauthor of *Productivity Revisited: Shifting Paradigms in Analysis and Policy; World Development Report 2019: The Changing Nature of Work;* and *Inclusive Global Value Chains: Policy Options for Small and Medium Enterprises and Low-Income Countries*. Her coauthored work has been published in the *Review of Economics and Statistics, Journal of Development Economics, World Bank Economic Review, Journal of Economics and Public Finance, Journal of Banking and Financial Economics, IZA Journal of Labor and Development,* and *Journal of Development Effectiveness*. Before joining the World Bank Group, she worked for the Inter-American Development Bank as a country economist and for the government of Argentina. She holds a PhD in economics from Universitat Pompeu Fabra.

Clément Gévaudan works with governments and international organizations to help strengthen science and innovation ecosystems. He supports the World Bank Office of the Chief Economist for the Middle East and North Africa to produce flagship knowledge products analyzing digital transformation in the region. He also engages with the Digital Development Global Practice, as well as the Finance, Competitiveness, and Innovation Global Practice, to achieve the World Bank's ambitious digital agenda. Throughout his career, he has collaborated with a wide network of specialized firms, research institutions, and public agencies in Africa, Asia, and Europe. In March 2018, he codirected the Global Development Conference, "Science, Technology, and Innovation for Development," in New Delhi, India. He is a development economist who graduated from Centre d'Études et de Recherches sur le Développement International (CERDI), a research center on international development based at the Université Clermont Auvergne in Clermont-Ferrand, France.

Daniel Lederman is lead economist and deputy chief economist for the Middle East and North Africa Region of the World Bank Group. Previously, he served as deputy chief economist for Latin America and the Caribbean, lead trade economist, senior economist in the Development Research Group, and senior economist and economist in the Office of the Chief Economist for Latin America and the Caribbean. He has written extensively on a broad set of issues, including financial crises, crime, political economy of reforms, economic growth, innovation, international trade, and labor markets. His research has been published in the *American Economic Review, Journal of Law and Economics, American Journal of Agricultural Economics, European Economic Review, Journal of International Economics, Journal of Development Economics*, and *Journal of International Business Studies*, among others. He has authored or coauthored several books, including *The Political Economy of Protection: Theory and the Chilean Experience; From Natural Resources to the Knowledge Economy*; and *Does What You Export Matter?*

Christina A. Wood is senior economist in the World Bank's Office of the Chief Economist for the Middle East and North Africa. Previously she was senior economist for Mali and Togo, and senior economist in the Office of the Chief Economist for East Asia and the Pacific. She has also worked on India. She has extensive experience leading multisector development policy lending and analyses covering a range of issues, including corporate governance (in banking, electricity, and commodity and natural resources), trade and transport facilitation, public expenditure management, and postconflict recovery and reconstruction. She is coauthor of several books, including *Trading Together: Reviving Middle East and North Africa Regional Integration in the Post-Covid Era; East Asia: Recovery and Beyond; Mali: From Sector Diagnostics toward an Integrated Growth Strategy*; and *Mali: Expanding and Diversifying Trade for Growth and Poverty Reduction*. Her coauthored research is published in *International Economics and Economic Policy* and *Journal of Development Studies*. She holds a BA Honors in economics from McGill University and pursued her doctoral studies in economics at Cornell University.

Executive Summary

The argument that digitalization helps to sustain economic activity has never been more obvious than during the crisis brought about by the global COVID-19 pandemic. Of note, digital technologies are general-purpose technologies that are used across a wide variety of economic activities. Consequently, the gains from achieving universal coverage of digital services are likely to be large and widespread across the economy.

This report argues that the Middle East and North Africa region is suffering from a "digital paradox": the region's use of social media accounts is high relative to what would be expected given its level of gross domestic product (GDP) per capita—an indicator of economic development—yet its use of digital tools, such as the internet, to make payments is low.

The good news is that the socioeconomic upside of digitalizing the economy of countries in the Middle East and North Africa (and other low- and middle-income economies) is probably huge. GDP per capita could rise by more than 40 percent, manufacturing revenues per unit of factors of production could rise by 37 percent, employment in manufacturing could rise by 7 percent, and tourist arrivals could rise by 70 percent, creating jobs in the hospitality sector. Long-term unemployment rates could fall to negligible levels, and female labor force participation could double to more than 40 percent.

The main explanation for the upside is that digital technologies reduce informational costs that constrain economic transactions. The report provides three concrete examples of this mechanism at work. The first example describes how data from digital platforms provide information about the quality of ride-hailing service providers, overcoming information asymmetries between drivers and riders and contributing to improved service quality over time. The second example describes the role of digital technologies, specifically, information and communication technologies (ICTs), in enabling firms in West Bank to overcome physical barriers to mobility. The third example highlights tourism service providers' use of the internet to disseminate information, which has the effect of reducing the barriers to travel posed by distance, language differences, and absence of a common border between origin and destination countries, thereby increasing demand for tourism services.

A key question is how fast the Middle East and North Africa can approach universal coverage of digital infrastructure and how the deployment of digital infrastructure services should be targeted. A second key question is how the region can achieve the widespread adoption of digital payment tools. Achieving widespread adoption of digital payments will require efforts to increase digitalization among the underserved, to enhance the functioning of financial and telecom sectors, and to build societal trust in the government and in related institutions such as banks and financial services firms. Achieving these objectives will require appropriate policies and programs that are implemented well.

Demand-side factors must be addressed in view of their role in determining the pace of digital adoption (or use) once digital coverage (or access) is attained. These factors include increased access to financial accounts (inclusion) and increased digital and financial literacy, which could be leveraged to expand digital finance networks. While efforts to expand financial inclusion should continue via traditional bank accounts, mobile money holds promise for accelerating the adoption of digital payments across society. The report finds that mobile money could spur digital payments, which would enable the region to overcome the constraint of low access to bank accounts and to digital products (credit cards) reliant on bank accounts.

The report offers a policy agenda covering three foundational pillars of the digital economy: digital infrastructure, digital payments, and regulations for e-commerce. While the foundational pillars are necessary for the digital economy to grow, they are by no means sufficient, as underscored by the region's digital paradox and its ICT levels being broadly comparable to those of other regions with regard to coverage (access), cost of services, and download speeds, particularly for mobile broadband services. Rather, the region's digital infrastructure constraints are more likely linked to conditions in the telecom sector. The analysis shows the importance of fostering liberalization and competition in telecom markets, which in turn requires granting independence to the telecom regulatory authorities.

Lower-than-expected use of digital payments is not correlated with the banking sector's regulatory restrictions in and of

themselves. For the rest of the world, the use of digital payments falls as banking sector restrictions increase and rises as the size of the banking sector's assets increases. Yet, the reverse pattern is observed in the Middle East and North Africa, suggesting that impediments to the growth of digital payments are structural but not explained by stringent regulations of the banking sector or by development (size) of the banking system.

Constraints in the banking sector likely lie in characteristics such as noncontestable markets and high shares of state-owned enterprises, although the report does not provide direct evidence of this effect due to data limitations for empirical analysis. Further review by financial and banking sector specialists is warranted to better understand what the structural impediments may be.

New data indicate that the region has an important reform agenda to pursue with regard to the regulatory framework for e-commerce, particularly with respect to consumer protection, data protection, and cybersecurity. Middle-income countries (MICs) in the Middle East and North Africa are comparable to MICs in other regions except in the areas of electronic signature, data privacy protections, online consumer protections, and cybersecurity. In contrast, high-income countries (HICs) in the Middle East and North Africa compare well with HICs in other regions in terms of electronic documents and e-signatures but lag with respect to all other regulatory areas. Whether these important regulatory factors constitute binding constraints on the use of digital payments remains an open question empirically.

Lastly, the massive amount of social and economic digital data being generated poses challenges and risks stemming from how the data are accessed, safeguarded, processed, and deployed. Use of digital data can be guided by an effective data governance framework that instills trust in digital information flows and mitigates the risks posed by digital technologies, including anticompetitive practices by dominant digital platform firms, weak protection of individuals' data privacy, and spread of disinformation through social media.

Trust in using digital payments might be boosted quickly by implementing e-government mechanisms. E-government options—such as digital cash transfers, digitized payment mechanisms for public services, and shifts to e-procurement—hold great promise for facilitating the rapid expansion in use of digital money. If designed appropriately and implemented well, e-government could build familiarity and trust in the use of digital payments for commercial purposes.

Abbreviations

BRSS	Bank Regulation and Supervision Survey
B2C	business-to-consumer
FLFP	female labor force participation
GDP	gross domestic product
GDPR	General Data Protection Regulation
GFDD	Global Financial Development Database
GPT	general-purpose technology
GSMA	Global System for Mobile Communications Association
HICs	high-income countries
ICT	information and communication technology
ID4D	Identity for Development
IT	information technology
ITU	International Telecommunication Union
MICs	middle-income countries
PPP	purchasing power parity
TFPR	total factor productivity rate
WDI	World Development Indicators

Introduction | 1

The case for digitalizing economies has never been stronger. Above all, the COVID-19 pandemic has made the benefits of conducting contactless transactions starkly clear. Certain economic and public sector activities have been able to continue while also reducing the need for social interactions. Moreover, digital technologies are being deployed to improve health outcomes to varying extents around the world. Digital applications through mobile devices are being used to aid efforts to monitor and contain the spread of the disease. Cell phone location data are being used to monitor mobility and assess risks. Compliance and privacy considerations of mobile contact-tracing applications are of paramount importance for digital applications to work effectively, as they rely on enough uptake by the public. This realization highlights the importance of building public trust through transparent data governance practices. Nonetheless, the case for digitalization has never been manifested in real time as clearly as it has been during the pandemic.

Yet, as this report shows, the digital economy is not synonymous with the use of digital tools, such as the internet, even though they are related. The difference is in how society uses digital services and internet access. Some services serve social purposes, others serve economic purposes, and most serve both. The Middle East and North Africa region, however, is suffering from a digital paradox: for its level of development, measured by gross domestic product (GDP) per capita, the region has an excess in the use of social media (defined as the number of Facebook accounts) and a deficit in the use of digital payments (defined as the number of individuals who have made or received a digital payment). Hence, with regard to the resiliency of economic activity during the pandemic, the region seems to be weathering the crisis at a distance from its potential, with a few exceptions.

Perhaps more important than the digital paradox, income per capita has grown slowly in the Middle East and North Africa for a long time (Arezki et al. 2019). Few countries in the region have managed to grow faster than the median growth rate observed among economies at similar levels of development in the rest of the world during the 21st century. The demand for labor has not kept pace with the increase in the supply of educated youth, giving rise to high unemployment rates among educated youth, particularly women. Such high rates of unemployment add to the forgone national income implied by the persistence of low female labor force participation.

1

Countries in the region have pursued various growth strategies, including inward-oriented import substitution; use of windfalls from oil exports to finance public investment projects; creation of special economic zones; large public sector construction projects; opening up to the global economy for trade and investment; and efforts to diversify away from oil. These strategies have met with varying yet limited success, as evidenced by the comparatively low economic growth rates achieved during at least the past 20 years. The latest potential source of growth—the digital economy—holds promise for accelerating growth and job creation, particularly for tech-savvy youth and educated women (Belhaj and Arezki 2019).

Given its relatively high coverage of digital technology infrastructure (especially mobile) and internet use for its income level, the region should be well on its way to achieving an advanced digital transformation—engaging in market transactions using internet and telecommunications applications that enable market interactions at a distance (using internet-based digital platforms or communicating with clients via email or websites). The Middle East and North Africa has a few successful digital businesses (notably, Careem and Souq) and nascent or up-and-coming digital ecosystems (notably in Jordan, Lebanon, Morocco, Saudi Arabia, and the United Arab Emirates). Yet the rapid takeoff of digital transformation is not quite at hand. The reality is that the Middle East and North Africa, particularly the low- and middle-income economies of the region, is on a slow rather than a fast trajectory toward digital economic transformation. The question is why. This report argues that a lack of societal trust in government and the financial system is hindering the wider adoption of digital payment tools. Simply put, the region's obstacles on the road to a flourishing digital economy are more analog than digital.

Before moving to the substance of the argument, it is useful to have a clear definition of digital technologies. Throughout, this report refers to digital technologies as data-driven general-purpose technologies that reduce the costs of economic and social interactions. For the purposes of this report, digital technologies mean an internet connection through high-speed fixed or mobile broadband, digital payment capabilities, and digital platforms that serve as matchmakers, allowing distanced users to connect more readily with each other (Evans and Schmalensee 2016). This report investigates and advocates for the benefits of using digital technologies and documents how accelerated development of the digital economy can lead to a flourishing and more inclusive economy in the region.

The rest of the report is organized as follows. Chapter 2 presents the evidence of the "digital paradox" and explains why general-purpose technologies such as digital tools are expected to have economywide benefits. Chapter 3 provides a framework for understanding the interactions between the development of digital infrastructure, use of digital tools, and societal trust in government. Chapter 4 presents evidence of how digital technologies can help to overcome market frictions, summarizing evidence concerning the impact of digitalization on information flows from ride-hailing platforms, on overcoming barriers to physical mobility, and on demand for tourism services. Chapter 5 presents the analytical framework and results concerning the impact of digitalization on GDP per capita, revenue productivity of formal manufacturing enterprises, labor market outcomes, and tourism flows. Chapter 6 discusses three pillars of the digital economy—digital infrastructure services, digital payment systems, and a regulatory framework for e-commerce. Chapter 7 addresses the challenges and risks associated with the rise of the digital economy—namely, issues related to competition among providers of digital services, potential risks associated with social media, and data governance. Lastly, chapter 8 summarizes the main findings, policy implications, and avenues for future research. Three appendixes provide technical details.

References

Arezki, Rabah, Daniel Lederman, Amani Abou Harb, Rachel Yuting Fan, Ha Nguyen, and Marwane Zouaidi. 2019. "Reforms and External Imbalances: The Labor-Productivity Connection in the Middle East and North Africa." MENA Economic Update, April 2019, World Bank, Washington, DC. https:// openknowledge.worldbank.org/handle /10986/31445.

Belhaj, Ferid, and Rabah Arezki. 2019. "The Middle East and North Africa Cannot Miss the Fourth Industrial Revolution." *Arab Voices* (blog), March 19, 2019. https://blogs .worldbank.org/arabvoices/middle-east-and -north-africa-cannot-miss-fourth-industrial -revolution.

Evans, David S., and Richard Schmalensee. 2016. *Matchmakers: The New Economics of Multisided Platforms*. Boston, MA: Harvard Business Review Press.

The Digital Paradox in the Middle East and North Africa and the Upside of Digital Technologies | 2

Technology use in the Middle East and North Africa region is characterized by a digital paradox. Whatever the reasons for the slow growth of the region's digital economy, it clearly is not merely a question of insufficient coverage of information and communication technology (ICT) infrastructure, slow internet speeds, or insufficient access to the internet. Notably, while the use of social media per capita in countries in the region outperforms that in other countries at comparable levels of gross domestic product (GDP) per capita, the use of digital payments underperforms that of comparator countries (figure 2.1). This divergence in the use of technology for social versus economic purposes is unique to all Middle East and North African countries, irrespective of GDP per capita. Econometric estimations indicate that, on average, the excess number of active Facebook accounts relative to the region's level of income is about 8 percent. In contrast, on average, the region's deficit in terms of the population's experience with making or receiving a digital payment is about 15 percent.[1] Yet without wider diffusion of digital payments, the region's digital economy will remain nascent.

Digital tools such as the internet, associated user applications, and other ICTs are general-purpose technologies (GPTs). Like other GPTs, such as electricity, telephones, and railroads, digital-economy technologies are usable across all sectors and boost economic connectivity—whether physical or virtual. According to Jovanovic and Rousseau (2005), as GPTs get better over time, they reduce costs and spur innovations beyond their initially imagined applications, products, and processes in many sectors. In doing so, they engender widespread gains throughout the economy. Indeed, the economic benefits tend to increase as GPTs become widely adopted. For example, digital platforms turbocharge the GPT characteristics of digital technologies, particularly network externalities that serve as a driving force of efficiency and productivity gains (Evans and Schmalensee 2016). The adoption of digital technologies is also associated with employment generation by enterprises, even in traditional manufacturing industries and even when the job gains are biased in favor of skilled workers. Firm-level evidence suggests that this association holds in emerging markets in Latin America (Dutz, Almeida, and Packard 2018). In addition, Hjort and Poulsen (2019) estimate that the arrival of high-speed internet submarine cables to Africa is associated with a significant increase in the probability of employment in local labor markets, ranging from 3 percent to

FIGURE 2.1 **Penetration of Facebook Accounts and Use of Digital Payments, by Region**

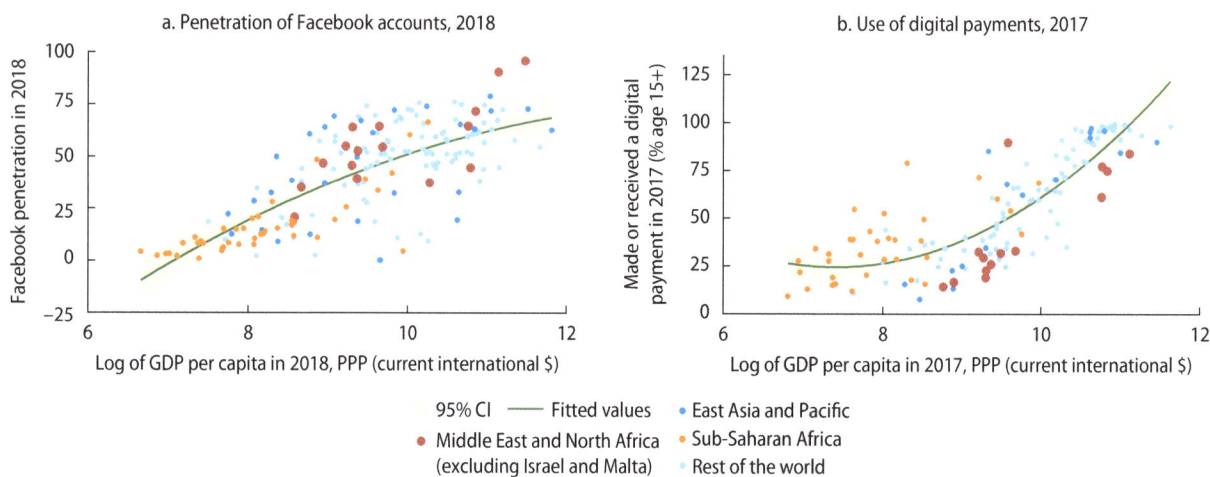

Sources: Computations based on data from Facebook, World Development Indicators (World Bank 2017b), and the Global Financial Inclusion (Findex) database (World Bank 2017a).
Note: The graphs show the empirical relationship between the level of development (measured along the horizontal axis by the log of GDP per capita adjusted for purchasing power parity in US dollars) and the number of active Facebook accounts per capita (panel a) and the share of the adult population reporting having made or received digital payments (panel b). The fitted curves in both panels show the best-fitting estimate of the relationship—namely, a quadratic function. Red dots correspond to observations from the Middle East and North Africa. Econometric estimates—not reported—indicate that the average vertical distance between the red dots and the fitted line is approximately +8% on panel a and −15% on panel b. CI = confidence interval. PPP = purchasing power parity.

13 percent, depending on the country and data set. In addition, they find that the arrival of high-speed internet is associated with an average increase in firm-level productivity of about 12.7 percent in manufacturing firms in Ethiopia. New empirical research indicates that such effects are similar in magnitude for countries in the Middle East and North Africa and for other low- and middle-income countries.

In view of the scale effects of ICTs, combined with their general-purpose applicability, a bold policy approach is desirable to increase access to the internet rapidly, improve the reliability and affordability of internet access, and enable the widespread diffusion and use of digital payment systems. However, the pace of digital technology adoption, as with other technologies, can vary across countries and space, depending on the speed with which the coverage of affordable digital infrastructure services expands across territories. A long-standing literature discusses the pace of technology adoption, ranging from agricultural production techniques in the 1950s to digital technologies today.[2] The empirics discussed here rely on assumptions about the speed of adoption based on what is observable in recent data. More specifically, the speed of adoption

is assumed to be equal to the typical or median percentage increase in the digital variable of interest. This annual adoption rate is further assumed to be the same across all countries. That is, the share of the unserved population falls by the median rate observed in the data.

In addition, transparency, accountability, and trust in digital technologies and data use are the indispensable complements for realizing the promise of digital transformation. The reason is simple: for society to adopt the widespread use of digital technologies to conduct economic transactions, users have to trust the regulatory environment, the financial or banking institutions, and the government itself. Otherwise, the societal adoption of digital payment systems will remain low even if the population has broad access to the internet and mobile telephony services. In this light, the region's digital paradox might be characterized as being due to gaps in societal trust.

Figure 2.2 provides suggestive evidence linking data transparency, trust, and digital payments, showing that some countries enjoy higher trust in politicians than expected for their level of data transparency, while other countries have lower public trust in politicians than expected for their level of data transparency. Consistent with the digital paradox,

FIGURE 2.2 **Correlation between Transparency, Trust, and Use of Digital Payments Worldwide**

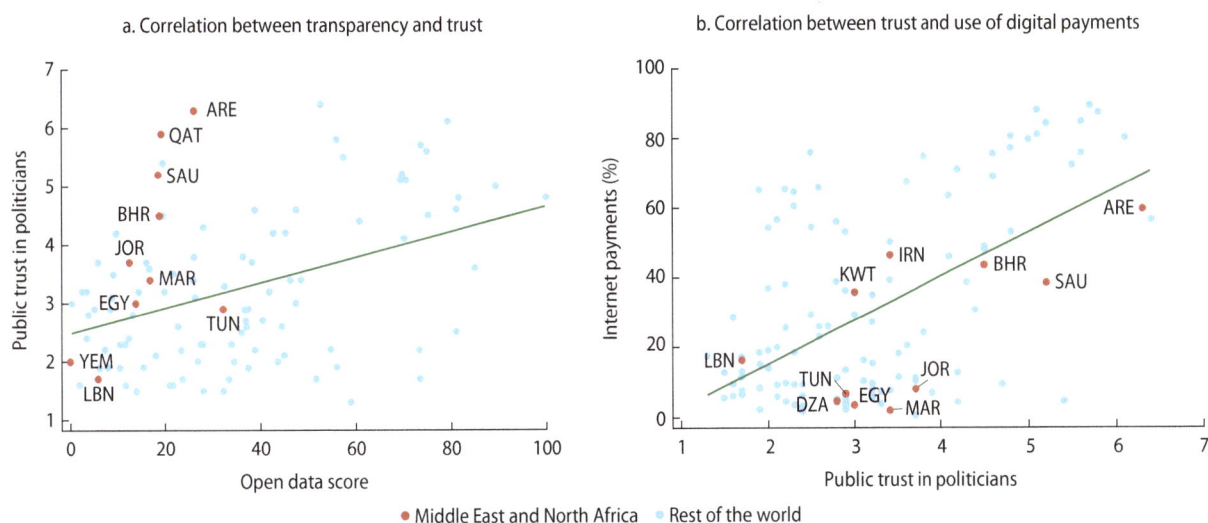

a. Correlation between transparency and trust

b. Correlation between trust and use of digital payments

● Middle East and North Africa ● Rest of the world

Sources: For panel a, data from Open Data Barometer (World Wide Web Foundation 2017) and World Economic Forum 2017. For panel b, data from Global Findex database (World Bank 2017a) and World Economic Forum 2017.
Note: The variables in the y-axis of panel a and the x-axis of both panels a and b are in scores without units. Internet payments refer to the response to "used the internet to pay bills or to buy something online in the past year (% age 15+)." The "public trust in politicians" indicator is for 2017; the "open data" indicator used is Open Data Barometer score scaled for 2016; and the "internet payments" indicator is for 2017.

most countries in the Middle East and North Africa have lower digital payments than expected for their level of public trust in politicians. This suggests that low trust is only one of several factors hampering the increased adoption of digital payments. Chapter 3 provides a framework for thinking about how policies and societal trust can shape the coverage of digital services, the use or adoption of digital tools such as digital payments, and the consequent socioeconomic implications.

Notes

1. The econometric results are reported in appendix B, along with tables of data on indicators of information technology infrastructure, finance, private sector technology adoption, and quality of institutions.
2. See, for example, Arezki et al. (2019); Griliches (1957); Jovanovic and Rousseau (2005); Juhász, Squicciarini, and Voigtländer (2020).

References

Arezki, Rabah, Daniel Lederman, Amani Abou Harb, Rachel Yuting Fan, Ha Nguyen, and Marwane Zouaidi. 2019. "Reforms and External Imbalances: The Labor-Productivity Connection in the Middle East and North Africa." Middle East and North Africa Economic Update, April 2019, World Bank, Washington, DC. https://openknowledge .worldbank.org/handle/10986/31445.

Dutz, Mark A., Rita K. Almeida, and Truman G. Packard. 2018. *The Jobs of Tomorrow: Technology, Productivity, and Prosperity in Latin America and the Caribbean.* Directions in Development. Washington, DC: World Bank.

Evans, David S., and Richard Schmalensee. 2016. *Matchmakers: The New Economics of Multisided Platforms.* Boston, MA: Harvard Business Review Press.

Griliches, Zvi. 1957. "Hybrid Corn: An Exploration in the Economics of Technological Change." *Econometrica* 25 (4): 501–22.

Hjort, Jonas, and Jonas Poulsen. 2019. "The Arrival of Fast Internet and Employment in Africa." *American Economic Review* 109 (3): 1032–79.

Jovanovic, Boyan, and Peter L. Rousseau. 2005. "General Purpose Technologies." NBER Working Paper w11093, National Bureau of Economic Research, Cambridge, MA. https:// ssrn.com/abstract=657607.

Juhász, Réka, Mara P. Squicciarini, and Nico Voigtländer. 2020. "Technology Adoption and Productivity Growth during the Industrial Revolution: Evidence from France." NBER Working Paper 27503, National Bureau of Economic Research, Cambridge, MA.

World Bank. 2017a. The Global Financial Inclusion (Findex) (database). Washington, DC: World Bank. https://globalfindex .worldbank.org/.

World Bank. 2017b. World Development Indicators (database). Washington, DC: World Bank. http://datatopics.worldbank.org/world -development-indicators/.

World Economic Forum. 2017. *The Global Competitiveness Report 2017–2018*. Geneva: World Economic Forum. https://www.weforum.org/reports /the-global-competitiveness-report-2017-2018.

World Wide Web Foundation. 2017. *The Open Data Barometer Global Report (Fourth Edition)*. Washington, DC: World Wide Web Foundation. http://www.opendatabarometer.org.

Framework for Understanding the Upside of the Digital Economy | 3

Digital technologies can help to overcome informational frictions that hamper the functioning of markets. Yet developing a digital economy requires establishing an enabling regulatory environment that creates the right incentives not only for the development of digital infrastructure (coverage, affordability, quality), digital products and services, and digital marketplaces, but also for the adoption of digital tools such as digital payments. Figure 3.1 visualizes the complex interactions between the coverage of digital infrastructure, society's adoption of digital tools (particularly digital payments), and societal trust in government and public institutions.

Working from the bottom up, figure 3.1 notes that countries with underdeveloped digital economies are hampered by informational and other frictions that make economic transactions costlier than would be the case with the adoption of digital technologies. These frictions manifest as coordination problems among individuals and firms, owing to a lack of the technologies needed to share information in real time, communicate with each other at a fast pace, and synchronize their actions. These economies also have spare human and physical capital that can be integrated into the economy through the development of digital markets, creating new income-earning opportunities for the working-age population.

As figure 3.1 shows, developing a digital economy requires setting the right enabling conditions (regulatory framework) to build the digital infrastructure, foster the supply of digital goods and services, and facilitate the creation of digital marketplaces. Such a regulatory framework relies, primarily, on three pillars: (a) competition policy to ensure coverage and quality of digital services; (b) data governance to secure users' data privacy and protection; and (c) sound e-commerce regulations governing intermediate liability, protection of online consumer activity, e-documents, and e-signatures, which are needed to increase users' confidence and trust in conducting transactions online. Chapters 6 and 7 explore these issues in detail.

In addition, societal trust—among citizens, between citizens and their governments, between citizens and key institutions such as banks—is important for the development of a digital economy. On the one hand, distrust in government and the banking system can discourage citizens from adopting digital payments and connecting to digital platforms. On the other hand, distrust can encourage citizens to adopt social digital tools as a vehicle of empowerment for expressing their dissatisfaction. Increased use of social media platforms often reduces the costs of collective action, thereby raising a society's collective voice in the form of

FIGURE 3.1 **Framework for Understanding the Interactions between the Development of Digital Infrastructure, Use of Digital Tools, and Societal Trust in Government**

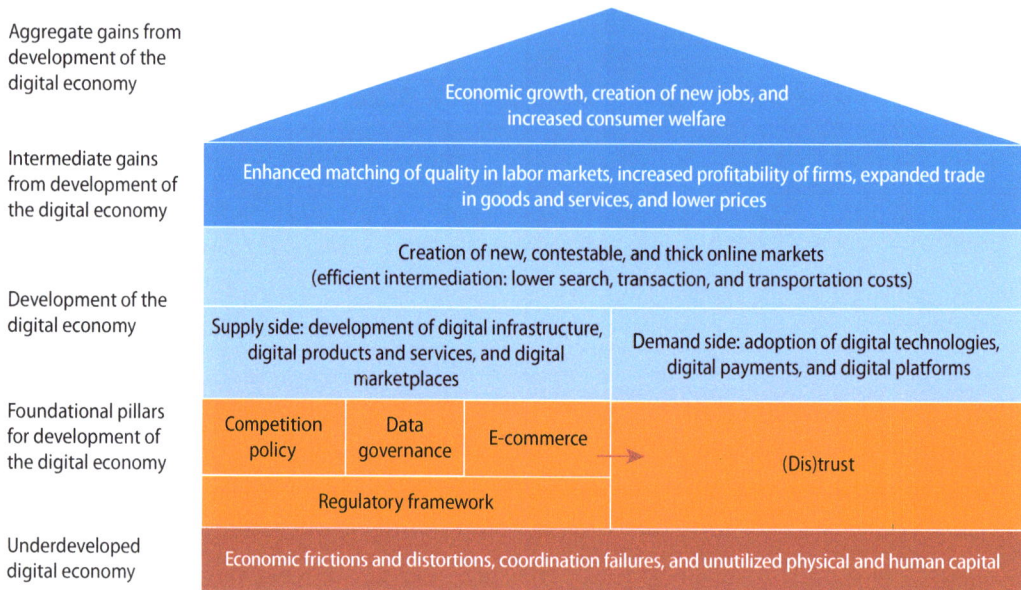

Source: Original figure for this publication.
Note: The terms "consumer welfare" and "consumer surplus" are used interchangeably to highlight the gains that consumers can obtain from a reduction in the price of products and services. Given the lack of information on demand for digital products and services and the inability to estimate the consumer surplus, the term "consumer welfare" is used to describe the benefits that consumers can enjoy from more competitive markets.

protests and other related phenomena (see Arezki et al. 2020; Fergusson and Molina 2019; Yee and Fassihi 2021). E-commerce regulations (discussed in chapter 6) play a role in fostering societal trust in conducting transactions online. Aspects of data governance (chapter 7) can also help build societal trust in participating in digital markets.

Societal trust is also affected by the use of digital technologies. The use of social media in and of itself has been found to increase distrust in government. Huang et al. (2020) find a negative relationship between the use of social media and trust in government, based on survey data from 20,667 respondents in 14 East Asian countries and territories. Furthermore, You and Wang (2020), using World Values Survey data, find that distrust is greater in countries with more authoritarian governments, reflecting a wider gap in those countries between the freedom of expression that individuals enjoy in using the internet and lack of freedom that they experience in interacting with their government.

You and Wang (2020) argue that their results provide evidence that authoritarian governments face greater challenges in overcoming the distrust of their citizens in the internet age.

Trust and use of digital payments also affect each other. The literature linking societal trust in government with use of e-government applications characterizes a multifaceted relationship that appears to be bidirectional, although the consensus leans toward a positive effect of trust on citizens' use of e-government (Mensah and Adams 2020). The few studies that analyze the reverse relationship find that e-government has a significant positive effect on trust, but only if e-government services improve government performance and transparency (Mahmood, Weerakkody, and Chen 2020; Song and Lee 2016).

Regarding the adoption of digital payments, Alkhowaiter (2020) reports the finding from 46 studies of data from Gulf Cooperation Council countries that the best predictors for adoption of digital payment and banking are trust, perceived security, and perceived usefulness of the payment or banking tool. Factors linking low trust to low adoption of digital payments or low use of internet banking, include high perceived risk (Balakrishnan and Shuib 2021, on the willingness of Malaysian ride-share drivers to go cashless), tax avoidance (Ligon et al. 2019, on small and medium merchants in Jaipur, India), and concerns over privacy (Png and Tan 2020, on the use of cash in retail transactions in 36 countries). As regards the Republic of Yemen, technology readiness and prior internet knowledge are found to have a positive effect on the adoption of digital payments, whereas risk does not have a significant effect (Alhakimi and Esmail 2020).

Once the supply and demand sides of the digital economy are developed, digitalization fosters efficient market intermediation through lower search, transaction, and transportation costs (see figure 3.1). The latter facilitates peer-to-peer transactions and taps into spare human and physical capital. As a result, digitalization not only enables the creation of new, contestable, and thick online markets, but also makes offline markets more competitive. Lower search, transaction, and transport costs improve the quality of matching in labor markets, increase the profitability of firms (as businesses use digital solutions like email to reduce marginal costs or business websites to scale up demand), expand the volume of trade, and make prices more competitive. Development of the digital economy thus boosts economic growth, facilitates the creation of new jobs, enhances consumer welfare, and offers a new development path for emerging economies. Chapter 4 spotlights three concrete empirical examples of how digital tools help to reduce the market frictions that hamper economic growth. Chapter 5 presents novel evidence about the economic gains that the Middle East and North Africa region can obtain by fostering development of the digital economy.

References

Alhakimi, Wail, and Jameel Esmail. 2020. "The Factors Influencing the Adoption of Internet Banking in Yemen." *International Journal of Electronic Banking* 2 (2): 97–117.

Alkhowaiter, Wassan Abdullah. 2020. "Digital Payment and Banking Adoption Research in Gulf Countries: A Systematic Literature Review." *International Journal of Information Management* 53 (August): 102102. https://doi.org/10.1016/j.ijinfomgt.2020.102102.

Arezki, Rabah, Alou Adesse Dama, Simeon Djankov, and Ha Nguyen. 2020. "Contagious Protests." Policy Research Working Paper 9321, World Bank, Washington, DC. https://openknowledge.worldbank.org/handle/10986/34130.

Balakrishnan, Vimala, and Nor Liyana Mohd Shuib. 2021. "Drivers and Inhibitors for Digital Payment Adoption Using the Cashless Society Readiness-Adoption Model in Malaysia." *Technology in Society* 65 (May): 101554. https://doi.org/10.1016/j.techsoc.2021.101554.

Fergusson, Leopoldo, and Carlos Molina. 2019. "Facebook Causes Protests." Working Paper CEDE 018002, Centro de Estudios sobre Desarrollo Económico, Universidad de los Andes, Bogotá, Colombia. https://repositorio.uniandes.edu.co/handle/1992/41105.

Huang, Yi-Hui Christine, Yuanhang Lu, Lang Kao, Christine Hiu Ying Choy, and Yu-tzung Chang. 2020. "Mainframes and Mandarins: The Impact of Internet Use on Institutional Trust in East Asia." *Telecommunications Policy* 44 (2): 101912. https://doi.org/10.1016/j.telpol.2020.101912.

Ligon, Ethan, Badal Malick, Ketki Sheth, and Carly Trachtman. 2019. "What Explains Low Adoption of Digital Payment Technologies? Evidence from Small-Scale Merchants in Jaipur, India." *PLoS ONE* 14 (7). https://doi.org/10.1371/journal.pone.0219450.

Mahmood, Mohamed, Vishanth Weerakkody, and Weifeng Chen. 2020. "The Role of Information and Communications Technology in the Transformation of Government and Citizen Trust." *International Review of Administrative Sciences* 86 (4): 708–28. doi:10.1177/0020852318816798.

Mensah, Isaac Kofi, and Samuel Adams. 2020. "A Comparative Analysis of the Impact of Political Trust on the Adoption of E-Government Services." *International Journal of Public Administration* 43 (8): 682–96. doi:10.1080/01900692.2019.1645687.

Png, Ivan P. L., and Charmaine H. Y. Tan. 2020. "Privacy, Trust in Banks, and Use of Cash." National University of Singapore, January 28, 2020. http://dx.doi.org/10.2139/ssrn.3526531.

Song, Changsoo, and Jooho Lee. 2016. "Citizens' Use of Social Media in Government, Perceived

Transparency, and Trust in Government." *Public Performance and Management Review* 39 (2): 430–53. doi: 10.1080/15309576.2015 .1108798.

Yee, Vivian, and Farnaz Fassihi. 2021. "Clubhouse App Creates Space for Open Talk in Middle East." *New York Times*, May 2, 2021. https://www.nytimes.com/2021/05/02 /world/middleeast/clubhouse-iran-egypt -mideast.html (accessed May 2, 2021).

You, Yu, and Zhengxu Wang. 2020. "The Internet, Political Trust, and Regime Types: A Cross-National and Multilevel Analysis." *Japanese Journal of Political Science* 21 (2): 68–89. doi: 10.1017/S1468109919000203.

How Digital Technologies Help to Overcome Market Frictions | 4

This chapter presents evidence of how digital technologies can help to overcome market frictions. The first example highlights how data from digital platforms provide information on the quality of service providers, thereby overcoming information asymmetries between drivers and riders in ride-hailing apps and contributing to improved service quality over time. The second example describes the role of digital technologies, specifically information and communication technologies (ICTs), in enabling information technology (IT) firms in West Bank to overcome barriers to physical mobility. The third example highlights tourism service providers' use of the internet, which has the effect of reducing the barriers posed by geographic distance and language differences and thereby increasing the demand for tourism services.

Overcoming Frictions due to Information Asymmetries on Ride-Hailing Platforms

Digital tools can either create new data or aggregate existing data into information that is useful to firms, consumers, and investors. On the firms' side, increased use of digital business solutions (for example, business email, website, e-platform connection) allows workers and managers to organize their work better and to access real-time information about their counterparts (for example, suppliers, customers, business partners), leading to an increase in firm productivity. Moreover, with the accumulation of customer reviews and the aggregation of experience ratings that are visible to all, the expectation overall is that firms engaged in the digital economy can develop their reputations and expand their customer base much more efficiently than entrants into traditional sectors.[1]

Digital tools, via dissemination of the increased data they generate, enable users to overcome frictions associated with information asymmetries in the marketplace. Online data-driven reputation systems have the potential to enhance trust in market transactions and increase market contestability, while allowing young firms to build on their early successes. An example is data from the ride-hailing company Careem (the Arab Republic of Egypt), which show how rider feedback may affect the quality of the driver pool and induce the quicker exit of some drivers (figure 4.1). Another example is data from Gojek (Indonesia), which illustrate how women in a conservative gender-norms context can still provide delivery services at higher rates than men (figure 4.2). These services are clearly an acceptable activity for women outside the home, providing them with income-earning opportunities.

FIGURE 4.1 Share of Drivers Working Each Week in the Arab Republic of Egypt, by Driver Quality, 2018

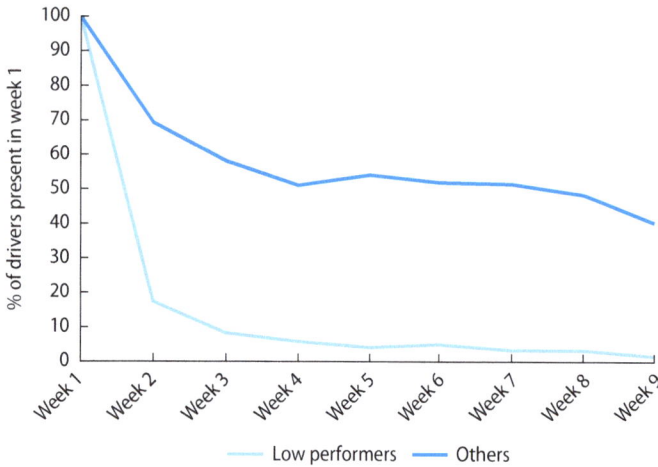

Source: Careem data for 2018.
Note: The figure represents the share of drivers present in the first week of the sample whose average score was less than three stars over the entire period (light blue line) or more than three stars (dark blue line).

FIGURE 4.2 Volume of Orders for Courier or Delivery Services in Jakarta, Indonesia, by Gender of the Driver, 2020

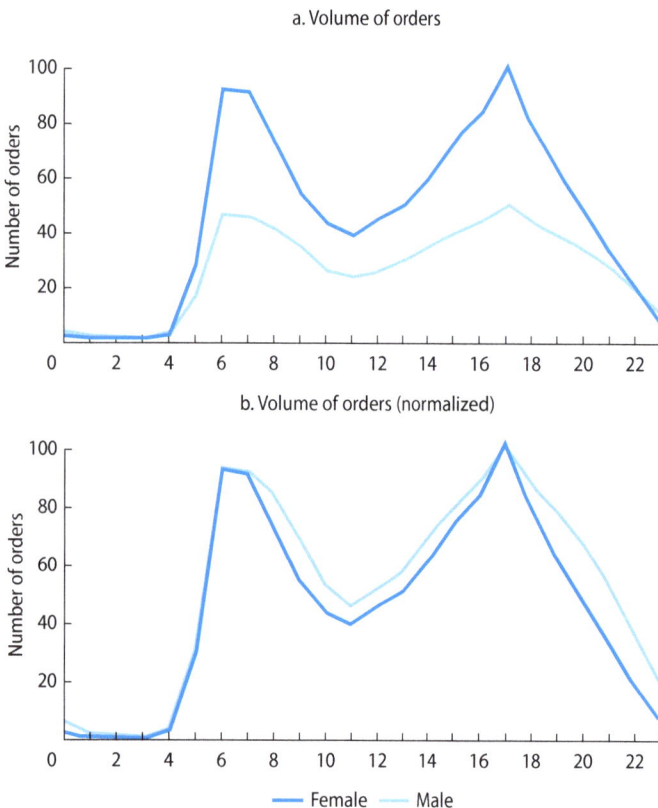

Source: Gojek data for 2020.
Note: The figures reflect data for two-wheel vehicles engaged mainly in courier and delivery services in the Greater Jakarta area.

Overcoming Transport Frictions: IT Sector and Mobility Barriers in West Bank

West Bank is a natural lab in which to explore the role of digital technologies in overcoming transport frictions arising from mobility restrictions, including a system of militarized checkpoints and roadblocks introduced since 2000 that impose heavy limits on the mobility of goods and people. Transport frictions are generally considered to be a significant barrier to growth, as they impose a high cost on the trade of goods. West Bank bears the effects of these barriers, with constrained growth of gross domestic product (GDP) and changes in the composition of economic activity.

A recent research study by Fratto and Giannone (2020) sheds light on the expansion of the IT sector and the stagnation of other sectors in the wake of mobility restrictions. The authors develop a multiple-industry model based on Eaton and Kortum (2002) to identify and describe the possible mechanisms that make the IT sector different from other sectors. They use a novel survey data set that captures information on more than 500 establishments representative of sectors of the West Bank economy, including IT, manufacturing, and retail. The data set combines information on geographic locations, travel times between locations, and mobility restrictions as well as data from population and establishment censuses, to identify the channels through which changes in market access can differentially affect industries.

Regarding expansion of the IT sector, Fratto and Giannone (2020) posit that, as the barriers to mobility weakened the incentives to invest in the production of physical goods, the opportunity cost of investing in IT also declined, raising the relative incentive to invest in IT. Indeed, by focusing on software development and website design, the IT sector's employment of the high-skill labor force allowed it to overcome the mobility restrictions. Fratto and Giannone (2020) find that mobility restrictions reallocated resources toward the IT sector, because it was relatively less affected by them. Indeed, the counterfactual exercise of removing mobility barriers was found to affect the IT sector disproportionately and adversely relative to other industries.

Table 4.1 reports the effects on GDP sector shares for the counterfactual scenario of reducing mobility barriers back to their 1995 levels. The easing of restrictions decreases the IT sector's contribution to GDP, from 12 percent to 7 percent, to the benefit of the manufacturing and retail sectors. Stated differently, as a result of mobility barriers, the IT sector's share of GDP was higher by 5 percentage points relative to 1995, while that of the manufacturing and retail sectors were each lower by about 10 percentage points.

The study further indicates that the IT sector in West Bank, while benefiting from an increase in the incentives to invest due to the mobility barriers, is still severely restricted by the local limitations. The sector relies on the presence of nearby clients, and strong input-output linkages limit its ability to grow in a constrained economy. This constraint is reflected in the data: IT sector employees tend to travel more for work (within West Bank) than non-IT sector workers, likely because IT sector activity has had to

rebalance toward software and repair of existing assets due to the constrained ability to import new equipment. In other ways though, the IT sector is similar to non-IT sectors in its inability to engage in cross-border trade via remote provision of IT services. The IT sector is overwhelming oriented to the domestic market, as are other sectors, because the restrictions on imports and exports affect all firms, regardless of industry.

The key role of input-output linkages (partly reflecting IT's characteristic as a general-purpose technology), the strong dependence on local clients and suppliers, and the deep interconnectedness with other domestic industries severely limit the extent to which the IT sector can benefit from the lower opportunity costs of investing in the sector. In the absence of input-output linkages, the increase in the IT sector's share of GDP that is associated with mobility restrictions would have been higher than 5 percentage points. Table 4.2 shows the simulated effects of reducing mobility restrictions on GDP growth and the influence of input-output linkages. In the absence of input-output linkages, easing the restrictions is

TABLE 4.1 **Change in Industry Shares of GDP in the Presence of Mobility Restrictions in West Bank, 1995–2017**

Sector component of GDP	Baseline model: Significant mobility restrictions (% of GDP)	Counterfactual: Reversion to 1995 mobility restrictions (% of GDP)	Change in industry sector shares due to mobility restrictions (percentage points)
Aggregate	100	100	0
Manufacturing	25	36	−11
Information technology	12	7	5
Retail	11	21	−10
Other	53	36	17

Source: Calculations based on Fratto and Giannone 2020, table 14.

TABLE 4.2 **Simulated Change in GDP in the Presence of Mobility Restrictions**

Sector component of GDP	With no input-output linkages (% change)	With input-output linkages (% change)	Impact of input-output linkages (percentage points)
Aggregate	0.25	1.16	0.91
Manufacturing	0.27	1.31	1.04
Information technology	0.05	0.78	0.73
Retail	0.32	2.06	1.74
Other	0.24	0.98	0.74

Source: Calculations based on Fratto and Giannone 2020, table 15 and appendix table 7.

estimated to increase GDP by 0.25 percent, corresponding to a 0.05 percent growth in the IT sector. Other sectors would grow much more, at least as much as GDP. With input-output linkages, however, GDP growth would have been 1 percentage point higher, and the IT sector's growth would have been about 0.73 percentage point higher.

Tourism Demand: Overcoming Frictions Associated with Geography and Language Barriers

Demand for tourism is a function of the cost of tourism services, as determined by distance, language, and a common border, among other factors. Extending the standard gravity model of trade in goods (Anderson and van Wincoop 2003) to tourism services trade, the literature finds the cost of tourism services to be higher when, relative to the origin country, the destination country is geographically farther, has a different language, and docs not share a common border. A consequence of the higher costs of tourism services is a decrease in the demand for destination-country tourism services by travelers in the country of origin.

Digital technologies are expected to affect the demand for tourism services to the extent that they affect costs. Adding digital

variables to the gravity model, Lopez-Cordova (2020) finds that increased internet use in either the origin or destination country, or in both countries, lowers the cost of searching, planning, and taking trips and hence increases the demand for a wider range of destinations relative to the baseline, including destinations that are farther away or less similar to the origin country.

The increased use of digital technologies eases the effort of acquiring information about travel destinations and planning trips, and also lowers the cost of traveling to those destinations. To assess the effect of digital technologies on tourism,[2] Lopez-Cordova (2020) proxies digital technologies with dummy variables reflecting population-wide internet use in the origin country[3] and business-to-consumer (B2C) internet use in the destination country.[4] Figure 4.3, panel a, presents the results, showing that the adoption of B2C tools has a greater impact on demand for tourism services than the baseline specification. In other words, the adoption of B2C tools eases the barriers associated with geographic distance, language differences, and absence of a common border, enabling demand for tourism services to increase by 0.3 percentage point,[5] 3.2 percentage points, and 0.8 percentage point, respectively, relative to the baseline

FIGURE 4.3   Change in Demand for Tourism Services, by Determinant

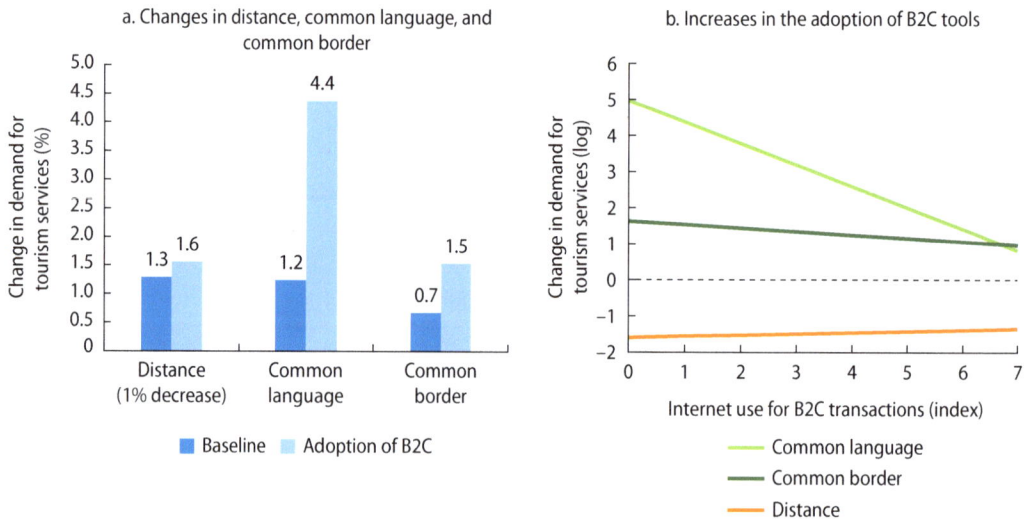

Source: Calculations using coefficients from Lopez-Cordova 2020, table 5(b), panel C, column 11, and baseline results in table 3, column 4.
Note: B2C = business-to-consumer.

model specification. Wider adoption of B2C further amplifies the effect of reductions in distance, while sharing a common border or a common language is a much less important determinant of demand for tourism services when B2C use is widespread (figure 4.3, panel b).

Chapter 5 presents the effects of reaching maximum B2C with a logit adoption schedule (fast technology adoption schedule) and quantifies the impact on the number of tourists and potential related jobs. That is, the adoption schedule follows an exponential path as more businesses adopt B2C tools. The magnitude of the upside of digital technology adoption depends on the initial level of B2C adoption (as of 2017, base year used in the simulation). The gains in tourist arrivals in the Middle East and North Africa are estimated to be about 70 percent higher relative to 2017, while the gains in employment are about 37 percent higher.

Notes

1. However, recent evidence shows that the reliability of the rankings based on consumer reviews is low, because consumers tend to post ratings and comments only when they are very pleased or very angry about a product. The bimodality in the distribution of reviews makes it difficult to infer where the true mean lies. Nonetheless, traditional markets provide no such feedback beyond observed market equilibrium prices.
2. The dependent variable is bilateral tourism flows from the United Nations World Tourism Organization (UNWTO 2019) and covers the period 1995 to 2017, the last available year of data. In contrast to trade data, reported tourism data vary considerably across countries. As such, the analysis uses arrivals of nonresident tourists or visitors at national borders as a proxy for demand for tourism services.
3. Reflected by the share of the population with internet access in the origin country, to approximate the extent to which would-be travelers can use digital tools for travel planning.
4. From the perspective of the destination country, this indicator captures the extent to which businesses use the internet to reach customers in the economy as a whole, not just in the tourism industry. The indicator ranges from 1 to 7 for responses to the survey question, "In your country, to what extent do businesses use the internet for selling their goods and services to consumers?"—with 1 being "not at all" and 7 being "to a great extent." The data are from the World Economic Forum's *Travel and Tourism Competitiveness Reports* (WEF 2015, 2017, 2019), with information dated two years prior to each report. As a result, in the first case, the econometric exercise uses only data for 2013, 2015, and 2017.
5. Destination countries that are geographically closer by 1 percent to the traveler's origin country result in a 0.3 percentage point increase in demand for tourism services.

References

Anderson, James E., and Eric van Wincoop. 2003. "Gravity with Gravitas: A Solution to the Border Puzzle." *American Economic Review* 93 (1): 170–92.

Eaton, Jonathan, and Samuel Kortum. 2002. "Technology, Geography, and Trade." *Econometrica* 70 (5): 1741–79.

Fratto, Chiara, and Elisa Giannone. 2020. "Market Access and Development of the ICT Sector in the West Bank." Policy Research Working Paper 9426, World Bank, Washington, DC. https://openknowledge.worldbank.org/handle/10986/34597.

Lopez-Cordova, Ernesto. 2020. "Digital Platforms and the Demand for International Tourism Services." Policy Research Working Paper 9147, World Bank, Washington, DC. https://openknowledge.worldbank.org/handle/10986/33352.

UNWTO (United Nations World Tourism Organization). 2019. *Compendium of Tourism Statistics* [electronic data set]. Madrid: UNWTO. Data updated on November 1, 2019.

WEF (World Economic Forum). 2015. *Travel and Tourism Competitiveness Report 2015*. Geneva: WEF.

WEF (World Economic Forum). 2017. *Travel and Tourism Competitiveness Report 2017*. Geneva: WEF.

WEF (World Economic Forum). 2019. *Travel and Tourism Competitiveness Report 2019*. Geneva: WEF.

The Upside of Digital: Empirical Framework and Results | 5

As depicted in the analytical framework presented in chapter 3, the widespread adoption of digital technologies can bring substantial gains to an economy via several channels. The open question is how high the economic upside of the digital economy is in the Middle East and North Africa. This chapter presents empirical research linking the expansion of coverage of digital infrastructure services and the adoption of digital technologies to long-term gains in gross domestic product (GDP) per capita, manufacturing firm-level revenue productivity, tourism flows, and labor market outcomes.

The upside of the digital economy can be huge, particularly for economies with low diffusion of information and communication technology (ICT) and less-developed digital payment systems, consistent with the findings of the technology-diffusion literature (Comin and Mestieri 2013; Comin and Rovito 2008).

The empirical framework relies on the estimation and computation of two key parameters. First, is an estimate of the marginal effects of the adoption of digital technologies, or the increase in coverage of digital services, whichever might be the case. Second, is an assumption about the speed with which digital tools will be adopted

across the population that has yet to adopt digital tools or is without access to digital services. The product of the marginal effect times the speed of adoption provides an estimate of the economic gains of digital technologies over time.

Since digital technologies are general-purpose technologies (GPTs), it is reasonable to expect that the socioeconomic gains are diffused across the economy and not concentrated in a few sectors. Consequently, the analysis explores the gains across several variables of interest. This basic framework, with model specifications tailored to the economic variable being estimated and the nature of the data being used as dependent variables, underlies the analysis quantifying the gains from technology adoption on GDP per capita, firm productivity, tourism, and labor market outcomes. Box 5.1 summarizes the empirical framework and lists the variables of interest.

Lower-Bound Estimates of the Upside of the Digital Economy

The estimates of the gains from the digital economy are likely to be lower-bound estimates, for at least several reasons. First, historical data are used for both the dependent and explanatory variables, which implies that

BOX 5.1   Empirical Framework for Estimating the Upside of Digital Technologies

The following model is used to estimate the effects on outcomes of interest:

$$\Delta y = \beta \times \Delta X, \tag{B5.1.1}$$

where $\Delta X \equiv$ *speed* of technology adoption, with the median or typical rate being the "business-as-usual scenario," and X is capped at **universal coverage** $\rightarrow$ Upside is higher at lower initial X.

The model is estimated for different outcomes and digital economy variables (with color coding indicating which y and X variables go together in the respective model equations):

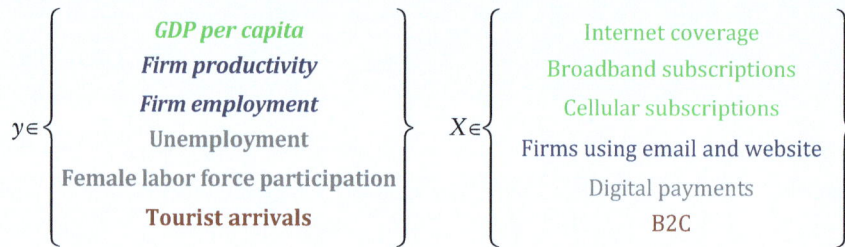

$$y \in \left\{ \begin{array}{c} \textit{GDP per capita} \\ \textit{Firm productivity} \\ \textit{Firm employment} \\ \text{Unemployment} \\ \textbf{Female labor force participation} \\ \textbf{Tourist arrivals} \end{array} \right\} \quad X \in \left\{ \begin{array}{c} \text{Internet coverage} \\ \text{Broadband subscriptions} \\ \text{Cellular subscriptions} \\ \text{Firms using email and website} \\ \text{Digital payments} \\ \text{B2C} \end{array} \right\}$$

Multiple ys and Xs require different estimation methods to estimate the marginal effect, β.

the estimates of the marginal effects (β in box 5.1) contain information about how recent digital technologies affected social and economic outcomes in the past. To the extent that new digital technologies—for example, 5G mobile data services are replacing 4G, which replaced 3G and 2G—are superior to the technologies observed in past data, the marginal effects could be higher than what is obtained from the econometric estimations using historical data.

Second, the explanatory variables (the Xs in box 5.1) are either proxies for the coverage of digital infrastructure services over a given population or proxies for the use of digital tools for economic purposes, such as survey data on whether adults report having used the internet to make a payment during the past year or month. To the extent that such proxy variables are measured with white-noise errors, the econometric estimates of β, the marginal effects, will suffer from attenuation bias.

There is one exception, however, which concerns a subset of the estimated gains for the formal manufacturing sector for one of two exercises. In that exercise, it is assumed that formal manufacturing enterprises could be "perfectly targeted" for digitalization. More precisely, this case focuses on the sector-wide gains in revenue productivity (or profitability) for all enterprises in which there are positive marginal effects. That is, the exercise includes only those enterprises for which $\beta > 0$. It is worth keeping in mind that, as enterprises begin to use digital tools, such as business websites and platforms, the market becomes more competitive as firms expand the scale of production. Consequently, prices can fall, reducing revenues for producers, but enhancing consumer welfare. In fact, Cusolito, Lederman, and Peña (2020) report that revenues do fall for a substantial portion of enterprises in low- and middle-income countries, although the median (or typical) marginal impact is positive. These ideas are explored further below.

Third, the speed of adjustment—the value of ΔX in box 5.1—is assumed to be slow. In a sense, the analysis applies a global business-as-usual scenario to all countries in the sample. As such, it is plausible that some countries could move faster, thus reaching the estimated gains much sooner than indicated by the models. Indeed, subsequent chapters discuss foundational policy areas for the digital economy precisely because the speed of increasing the coverage or the adoption of digital technologies is, to a large extent, a policy choice. More specifically, for each digital indicator, the model assumes that the rate of adoption is equal to the median rate of change in the population that either gains access to digital infrastructure services or adopts digital tools such as payments. This assumption has the advantage of illustrating how the upsides of digital vary systematically with the share of the unserved population, as of the latest year in the data sets. In other words, the results presented here differ across regions and countries only because the initial conditions are different, not because different rates of adoption are imposed.

Finally, the rate of increased coverage or adoption of digital tools is worth exploring because it plays a key role in determining the timing of realization of the gains. Figure 5.1 shows simulations of three schedules for adopting digital technologies. Each adoption

schedule has the same starting point and assumes the same rate of adoption from year to year. The only differences are the functional forms that link the outcome variable with the speed of adoption. More precisely, the three scenarios depicted in figure 5.1 assume that the hypothetical economy starts in 2017 with only 40 percent of the population having access to a given hypothetical digital service or tool. Also, the speed of adjustment is assumed to be 2.5 percent per year. The linear model of adoption simply assumes that the share of the served population advances by 2.5 percentage points each year. This approach is inconsistent because it predicts that the population with access to the digital service in question will exceed 100 percent of the national population in the out years of the simulation horizon, which is impossible.

The concave function in figure 5.1 is consistent with the literature on the speed of advance of infrastructure services, which is slowed by the fixed costs associated with infrastructure investments and the concomitant rising costs per customer—the last-mile problem. It implies a very slow pace of

FIGURE 5.1   **Simulated Schedules for Diffusion of Digital Technology, 2017–50: Linear, Concave, and Logit Functions**

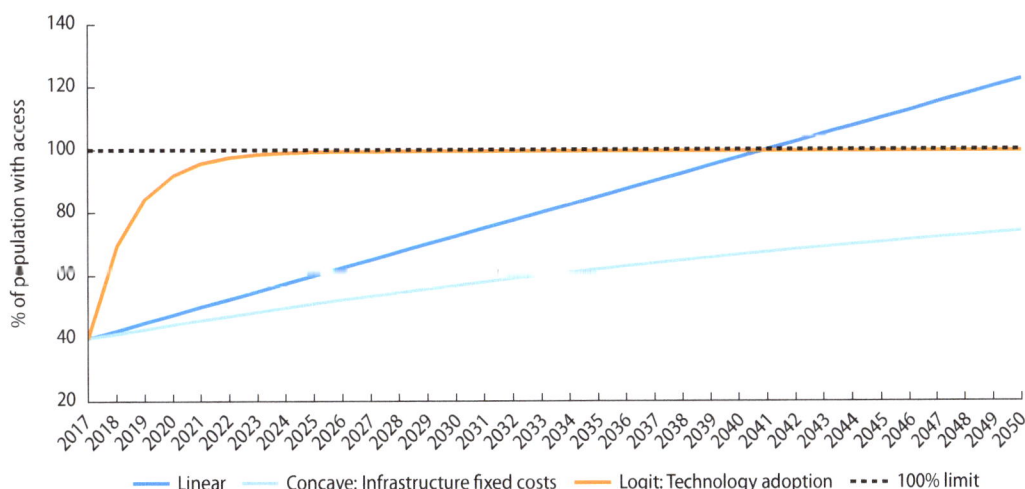

Source: Original calculations for this publication.
Note: Data are simulated and applied to a hypothetical economy. Initial condition: only 40% of the hypothetical country's population has access to a digital tool or service. The rate of adoption is 2.5% per year. The linear model assumes that 2.5% of the total population gains access each year. The concave model assumes that 2.5% of the *unserved* population gains access each year. This model is consistent with a slow uptake of infrastructure services when the expansion requires fixed investments and rising costs per customer. The logit model assumes a logit function, by which coverage increases at an exponential (by factor of 2.5%) rate as the coverage ratio approaches 100% of the hypothetical population. This model is consistent with the literature on technology adoption when the costs of adoption concern experimental costs by enterprises and individuals. But once the technology is well understood, the technology is adopted quickly by the initially unserved population. See, for example, Griliches (1957) and the main text for details.

increase in the share of the population with access to digital infrastructure services, but it is consistent in that the share never exceeds 100 percent.

The logit function in figure 5.1 is consistent with the literature on technology adoption, in which the adoption of a given technology requires experimentation costs at the beginning when few agents in the economy have adopted the technology. Afterward, when the adoption rate is well above zero, the adoption of the technology rises as an exponential function of the speed of adoption (which is also 2.5 percent per year, as in the other two examples). This type of function has been present in the technology diffusion literature at least since the publication of Griliches (1957). The difference between increases in the coverage of digital infrastructure services and the adoption of digital technologies is worth emphasizing.

In any case, the key point is that the magnitudes of the estimates discussed here need to be interpreted with a grain of salt, but it is likely that they underestimate both the total gains from achieving universal coverage and how fast those gains can be realized.

Gains in GDP per Capita

The lower-bound estimate for cumulative GDP growth is 46 percent for Middle East and North African countries as a whole and 71 percent for the region if high-income countries are excluded. Figure 5.2 shows that these gains accrue more quickly in the short term, but then accumulate more slowly as an economy approaches universal coverage. This is due entirely to the assumption concerning the speed with which internet use, mobile phone subscriptions, and broadband subscriptions spread across the population. The adoption schedule follows the concave function already described. That is, the fixed proportion of the unserved population as of 2017 is assumed to gain access at a rate of 2.4 percentage points for mobile phones, 0.5 percentage point for fixed lines, and 1.4 percentage points for internet use. So, more individuals gain access in the early years of the simulation exercise than in the later years.

In comparison with lower-income countries in Sub-Saharan Africa, the cumulative gains in income per capita are lower in the Middle East and North Africa. This is due

FIGURE 5.2   The Upside of Digital: Cumulative Gains in GDP per Capita in the Middle East and North Africa and in Sub-Saharan Africa, 2017–45

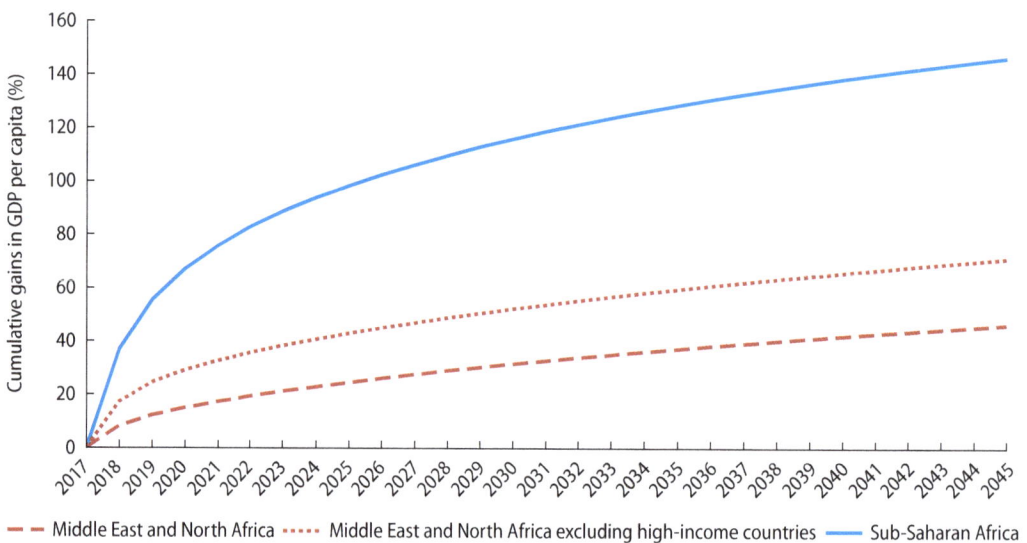

Source: Calculations based on estimates of the marginal effects of digital infrastructure on the level of GDP per capita presented in Calderon et al. 2019.
Note: The estimates of the marginal effects of expanding digital infrastructure services (internet use, mobile subscriptions, and broadband subscriptions) control for the preexisting level of GDP per capita and other indicators used in the various regression analyses. All countries are assigned the same marginal effect. The assumed adoption schedule follows the concave function discussed in the text. The data for each curve have been normalized to obtain start values of "0" in 2017.

entirely to the fact that in 2017 the Middle East and North Africa made digital infrastructure services accessible to a larger share of the population than did Sub-Saharan Africa (for selected indicators, see appendix B). This finding is by construction, since both the marginal effect and the speed of diffusion are assumed to be the same for the two regions. An important implication of this finding is precisely that economies starting from lower levels of digital technology penetration have a larger upside than economies in which significant portions of the population already have access to digital services.[1] From a policy perspective, logic dictates that focusing on bringing digital services to underserved countries or even underserved regions within countries will tend to pay off more than focusing on populations that already have access to such services.

The evidence discussed thus far needs to be weighed against the possibility that reaching universal access might be more costly per beneficiary in Sub-Saharan Africa than in the Middle East and North Africa. This would be the case, for example, if populations are less urban and more rural in Sub-Saharan Africa than in the Middle East and North Africa. The reason is that the cost per beneficiary of digital infrastructure tends to be higher in low-density populations. The same applies to rural populations within Middle East and North African countries.[2] In other words, figure 5.2 shows the gross gains in GDP per capita under conservative assumptions, but it does not take into account the costs per user that would be required to reach universal coverage in Sub-Saharan Africa or the Middle East and North Africa.

Gains in Revenue Productivity and Employment in Manufacturing

The literature has established that the adoption of digital technology increases the productivity of firms by allowing them to reduce costs, scale up operations, and create new jobs as digital tools allow them to reach a larger pool of potential customers and input suppliers. By narrowing the (virtual) distance between buyers and sellers in the economy,

and between job seekers and job creators, digital technologies expand market opportunities (De Loecker 2019). The reductions in search, transaction, and tracking costs allow firms to overcome geographic barriers, expand operations to existing clients, penetrate new markets, and enlarge the volume of trade (World Bank 2020). Using a sample of almost 8,000 formal manufacturing enterprises from across the world, Cusolito, Lederman, and Peña (2020) estimate the effects of technology adoption (website and email) on the performance of enterprises. They find that, for the typical (median) enterprise, the expected (probability-adjusted) gain in website adoption offers higher gains in revenue productivity (2.2 percent) than either exporting (1.7 percent) or upgrading managerial experience (0.05 percent). In addition, digital technology adoption is found to augment both labor and capital in the sense that the scale of production tends to increase in tandem with the increase in the adoption of digital technology, thereby also increasing the demand for labor and capital by firms.

However, the impact of digital technology adoption on the performance of enterprises is complicated by the fact that the effects tend to differ across enterprises. Cusolito, Lederman, and Peña (2020) show evidence suggesting that the gains in revenue productivity are higher for some firms than for others, depending on how productive they were before adopting a business website or whether they are exporters or not. More specifically, the evidence suggests that firms with lower productivity tend to experience higher marginal gains (the β parameter) than firms with higher levels of productivity to begin with. However, for exporting firms, the reverse is true: higher-productivity exporting firms tend to gain more from digital technology adoption than do lower-productivity exporters.

Figure 5.3 depicts the difference in revenue productivity effects following website adoption that are experienced by the typical (median) enterprise[3] and exporter, depending on its initial revenue productivity (that is, profitability) level. The typical enterprise (a non-exporter) with low initial profits is small (is a price taker) and thus, has minimal impact on the markets in which it operates.

FIGURE 5.3   **Digital Adoption and Export Complementarities: The Issue of Targeting**

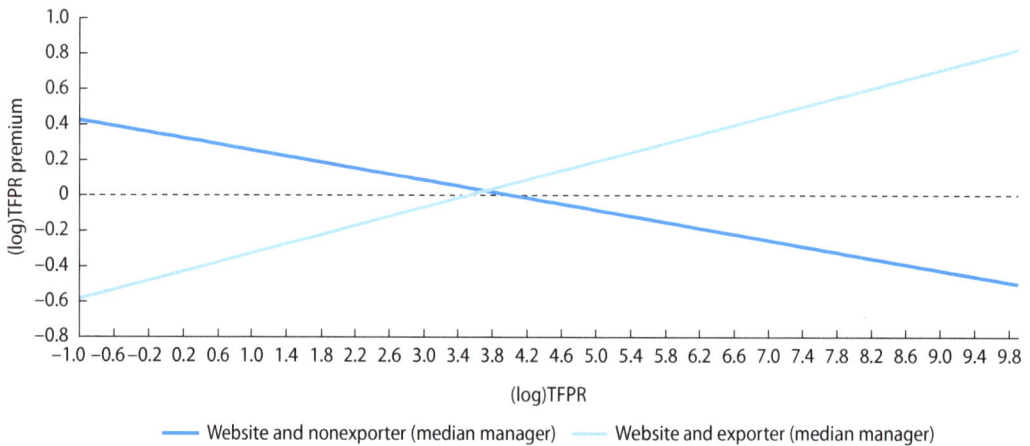

Source: Calculations using the estimated coefficients for median managerial experience in Cusolito, Lederman, and Peña 2020.
Note: The graph shows the marginal gains in TFPR from adopting a website for exporting and nonexporting firms. TFPR = total factor productivity rate.

When its scale of production increases due to website adoption (proxy of a demand shock), domestic prices do not fall much because of the firm's atomistic nature in the market, while production costs fall, yielding a net increase in the firm's profits. However, the domestically oriented firm is often large, with high initial profits. When this firm adopts a website, the resulting expansion in its scale of production drives down domestic prices, lowering the firm's profits notwithstanding the cost savings gained.

For an exporting firm, an increase in its scale of production (due to website adoption) has no impact on the output prices it faces (the firm is small relative to its export markets), although it may have an effect on the price of some of the inputs sourced in its home market. The exporting firm with initially low profits will experience a reduction in losses, as the increased scale of production (without an increase in output prices) increases its revenues, which may be amplified further in response to any decline in input prices. Similarly, an exporting firm with initially high profits will experience larger revenue gains than smaller exporters due to the likely larger response in output (at the same output price) and lower (domestic) input prices.

These differential effects between domestic and exporting firms suggest that, when website adoption is coupled with the goal of

increasing access to foreign markets, it may be better to target high-productivity exporting firms, given the high complementarities between digital technology business solutions and exporting. Furthermore, those complementarities are associated with higher gains in revenue productivity than if only one criterion is used to target firms for program support. Recent firm-level evidence highlights the relevance of making complementary investments and organizational innovations to help adopting firms take advantage of their newly adopted digital business solutions (Bresnahan, Brynjolfsson, and Hitt 2002; Brynjolfsson, Jin, and McElheran 2020; Brynjolfsson, Rock, and Syverson 2017).

An important policy issue emerges, therefore, because of the apparent heterogeneity in the marginal effects of digital technology adoption by manufacturing enterprises, which are reported by Cusolito, Lederman, and Peña (2020). If governments have limited resources for providing digital services to enterprises or training programs to entrepreneurs, the issue is which types of enterprises should be prioritized.

The results shown in figure 5.4 can help to guide the policy discussions about targeting. The figure shows the cumulative gains in revenue productivity (profitability) in the formal manufacturing sectors of both the Middle East and North Africa and Sub-Saharan Africa.

FIGURE 5.4 **Cumulative Gains in Revenue Productivity in Formal Manufacturing Enterprises in the Middle East and North Africa and in Sub-Saharan Africa, with Perfect Targeting and with No Targeting**

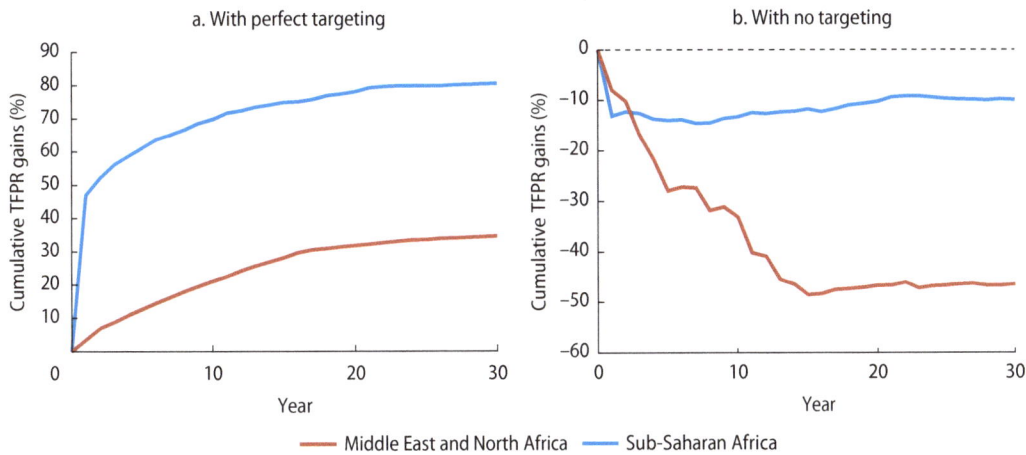

Sources: Calculations based on estimates from Cusolito, Lederman, and Peña 2020 and data from the World Bank Enterprise Surveys.
Note: Panel a shows a simulation of the gains in revenue-based total factor productivity accumulated in each region's formal manufacturing sector under the assumption that digitalization is perfectly targeted on enterprises with positive marginal effects. Panel b includes all enterprises, both those with negative marginal effects and those with positive marginal effects. The rate of adoption across enterprises is assumed to be concave, and the annual rate of adoption is 5%. This rate corresponds to the global average annual adoption rate calculated using the last two waves of the panel database for the econometric analysis. Adoption of a business website is assumed to target the lowest-productivity firms first. Each firm has its own marginal effect, depending on its characteristics, the most important ones being preadoption revenue productivity and exporting status. To expand the sample of countries for the simulation analysis, Cusolito, Lederman, and Peña (2020) use the last wave of the World Bank Enterprise Survey database. This wave includes a larger sample of Middle East and North African countries than that included in the econometric analysis, as several countries in the region have only cross-sectional (instead of panel) data and therefore could not be included in estimating the main digitalization effects. Counterfactual simulations for the Middle East and North Africa have been conducted for a sample of eight countries: the Arab Republic of Egypt, Iraq, Israel, Jordan, Lebanon, Morocco, Tunisia, and the Republic of Yemen. Regions are GDP- and PPP-adjusted weighted averages. Results with simple averages are available on request. See Cusolito, Lederman, and Peña (2020) for further technical details on the estimation of marginal effects across enterprises. The data for each region have been normalized to obtain start values of "0" in year 0. PPP = purchasing power parity. TFPR = total factor productivity rate.

The adoption schedule follows the concave function discussed earlier, but enterprises are ranked by their level of revenue productivity before adoption, from lowest to highest.[4] As mentioned, this exercise assumes that digitalization is perfectly targeted on enterprises with positive marginal effects, independent of their export status. For both regions, most of the gains are achieved in the early years. To the extent that the results reported in Cusolito, Lederman, and Peña (2020) are robust, this evidence suggests that most of the gains can be achieved quickly if lower-productivity firms are targeted first. Another important policy implication is that most of the upside gains in enterprise revenue productivity are associated with digitalization of the less advanced enterprises that do not export and the exporting enterprises that have the highest revenue per unit of factor of production (profitability) before digitalization, as reported in Cusolito, Lederman, and Peña (2020). These results are

consistent with the idea that domestic prices are likely to fall as nonexporting enterprises expand their production, with this effect being lower if the expanding firms are small. Hence targeting digitalization programs on the least advanced firms could yield the most gains in the shortest period.

When the digitalization exercise includes all enterprises—both those with negative marginal effects as well as those with positive marginal effects—the magnitude and trajectory of cumulative revenue productivity gains change markedly, as shown in figure 5.4, panel b. Firms may experience a reduction in profitability when the pro-competitive effects from digitalization on prices overcome the efficiency and scale-related gains. These pro-competitive effects are explained by lower search costs, as they facilitate price comparisons by consumers. The broad empirical literature examining the effect of digitalization on prices is summarized in Goldfarb (2020) and Goldfarb and Tucker (2019). The finding is that prices fall, and price dispersion generally falls—in online markets in high-income countries—even though price dispersion remains high.[5] Evidence about reductions in prices and price dispersion associated with lower search costs is even more compelling in low- and middle-income economies (Goldfarb 2020). This finding is explained mainly by the fact that new communication technologies are far more useful than existing infrastructure and that retailers lack the capabilities to manipulate search algorithms.[6] Figure 5.4, panel b, displays simulated revenue productivity gains from website adoption for the entire sample of nonadopters. As with the case of perfect targeting, both the Middle East and North Africa and Sub-Saharan Africa experience most of the gains in the early years of adoption. But in the case of adoption by all firms (not only those with positive marginal effects), the magnitude of the cumulative productivity gains in the early years is much lower than with perfect targeting, since the low gains in revenue productivity from the initially low-profit exporting firms partially offset the higher gains in profitability from the initially low-profit domestic firms. As time goes by, high-productivity firms are targeted and incorporated in the analysis. Since high-productivity firms often charge higher markups, these firms experience lower price reductions due to digitalization than low-productivity firms, a fact that explains the downward slope of the Middle East and North Africa curve in figure 5.4, panel b.

As enterprises adopt digital tools, such as business websites, their customer base is likely to expand. Consequently, it is possible that, in addition to improved efficiency, there might be gains in employment. In other words, the scale of production is likely to increase as the customer pool increases with the reach of digital tools. Cusolito, Lederman, and Peña (2020) explore this effect on enterprise-level labor demand.

To understand the rationale underlying the case for targeting lower-productivity enterprises, recall that the adoption of digital tools (such as websites) affects firm performance through three channels: (a) a pro-competitive effect, as the price of manufactured goods declines due to lower search costs, (b) an efficiency effect, as firms gain access to more competitive input providers, and (c) a scale effect, as firms can expand their base of potential customers. The evidence shows that profitability rises among low-profit enterprises that are not exporters. Profitability also rises among high-profit enterprises that are exporters. Thus, if a government chooses to maximize *profits* (in its manufacturing sector), the digitalization efforts could be targeted on low-profit firms that produce for the domestic market or high-profit firms that produce for external markets. However, if a government wishes to maximize consumer *welfare* rather than profits, then the optimal targeting would be the opposite. The scale effects appear to be nearly homogeneous across enterprises—that is, the magnitude of the effects is largely independent of a firm's profitability. Thus, if the objective is to create *jobs*, targeting is unnecessary.

Figure 5.5, panel a, shows the results of the simulations for employment generation in the formal manufacturing sector of the Middle East and North Africa and Sub-Saharan Africa when technology adoption is targeted at enterprises exhibiting gains in revenue productivity from website adoption. The aggregate effects tend to be larger for Sub-Saharan Africa than for the Middle East and North Africa because the initial share of enterprises that did not adopt websites was larger in the former than in the latter. For the Middle East and North Africa, this evidence suggests that achieving universal coverage of website adoption in the manufacturing sector would raise the probability of employment in the sector by about 6 percent; the corresponding impact in Sub-Saharan Africa would be around 8 percent. Of course, these estimates need to be interpreted with caution, due to the underlying assumptions of the model.[7] However, they appear to be within the range of estimates in the academic literature. Hjort and Poulsen (2019) report gains from the arrival of high-speed internet cables in Sub-Saharan Africa on the order of 7–13 percentage points in the probability of employment at the local level.[8] However,

FIGURE 5.5 **Employment Gains from Website Adoption in the Middle East and North Africa and in Sub-Saharan Africa, with Perfect Targeting and with No Targeting**

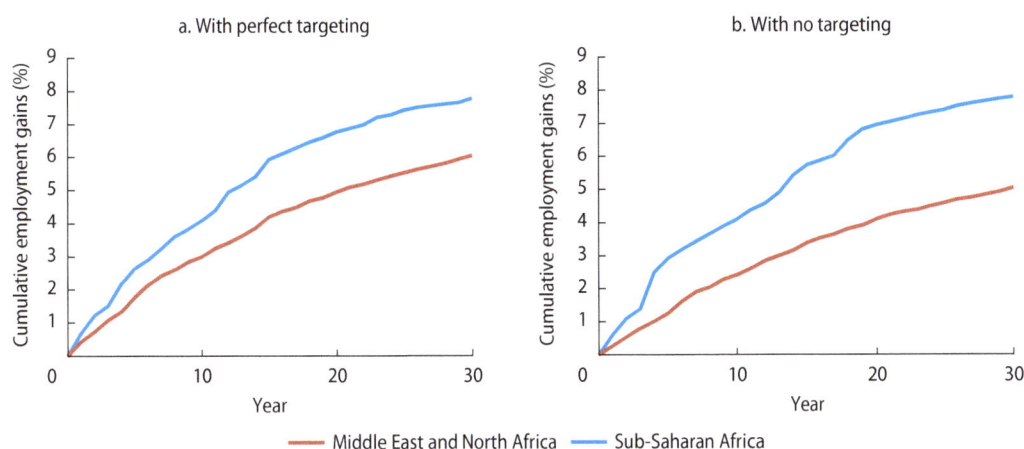

Source: Calculations based on estimates of marginal effects by Cusolito, Lederman, and Peña 2020.
Note: The graphs show the cumulative gains in employment in percentages relative to the scenario of no further website adoption than in the latest year of the World Bank Enterprise Surveys. The implicit annual adoption rate is 5%, which corresponds to the global average annual adoption rate calculated using the last two waves of the panel database used for the econometric analysis. The adoption schedule follows the concave function. Enterprises are ranked by their preadoption level of revenue-based productivity. Cusolito, Lederman, and Peña (2020) provide estimates of two marginal effects: a direct scale effect leading to increases in employment and the effect of website adoption on revenue productivity, which in turn affects employment. The latter effect is small but positive, implying that the productivity gains are labor-augmenting and that labor demand rises in response to the improvements in revenue-based productivity. The graphs show the simulated effects of the sum of both effects. The simulation results assume that the number of formal manufacturing enterprises in each country and region is fixed—that is, there is no entry or exit of enterprises. The Middle East and North Africa includes 10 economies: Djibouti, the Arab Republic of Egypt, Iraq, Israel, Jordan, Lebanon, Morocco, Tunisia, West Bank and Gaza, and the Republic of Yemen. Since data for estimating TFPR are not available for Djibouti or for West Bank and Gaza, the employment gains simulated for these two economies are a lower bound, as indirect effects through improvements in TFPR are not considered. Regions are GDP- and PPP-adjusted weighted averages. Results with simple averages are available on request. The data for each region have been normalized to obtain start values of "0" in year 0. PPP = purchasing power parity. TFPR = total factor productivity rate.

these scenarios assume that digitalization is perfectly targeted on enterprises with positive marginal effects on revenues. Given the estimated labor demand effects reported by Cusolito, Lederman, and Peña (2020), this scenario raises the cumulative impact on labor demand for the sector only slightly, because revenue gains have only a small positive impact on labor demand.[9] Indeed, when all of the sample of adopters is targeted, independent of the direction of the marginal effect on revenue productivity, employment gains decrease to 5 percent, approximately, for the Middle East and North Africa and to less than 8 percent for Sub-Saharan Africa (figure 5.5, panel b).

Gains in Tourism and Hospitality Industry Jobs

The adoption of digital technology also increases the activity in service sectors, such as tourism, that depend on bringing information about services offered in one country to potential customers residing in other countries (also discussed in chapter 4). Due to language differences and geographic distance between countries, potential tourists use the internet to help them to make travel choices. Hence, the extent to which national service providers, such as hotels and other businesses in the hospitality sector, have the digital tools to reach customers from far away, is important for the dynamism of the industry. For example, data from TripAdvisor on accommodations, attractions (for example, museums, tours), and eateries in Jordan doubled from a combined 1.25 million to 2.5 million "page views" per month between 2017 and 2019 (reported in Lopez-Cordova 2020). Over the same period, travelers to Jordan also increased their use of platforms such as Booking.com to arrange stays in both traditional (hotels) and nontraditional (bed and breakfast) establishments.

Lopez-Cordova (2020) provides preliminary econometric estimates of the potential effects of enhancing the coverage of business-to-consumer (B2C) digital tools on tourism arrivals. That study uses a well-established model in the literature on international trade—the gravity model of trade—to assess the drivers of tourist arrivals between pairs of countries. The estimates suggest that the coverage of B2C (proxied by the World Economic Forum index of B2C) tends to attenuate the impact of international differences in languages, borders, and geographic distance on bilateral tourism. By reducing the costs involved in breaking language barriers and reaching customers from faraway countries, the adoption of digital tools tends to increase tourism. Lopez-Cordova obtains similar results when using Google Trends data on the use of travel digital platforms such as TripAdvisor.

Figure 5.6 shows the implications for tourism in the Middle East and North Africa and in Sub-Saharan Africa of host countries reaching the top scores of the World Economic Forum's B2C scores. The adoption schedule follows the logit functional form described earlier. In other words, it assumes that adopting B2C strategies across the hospitality industry in each country is similar to

adopting technologies where the relevant infrastructure is already in place. That is, the adoption schedule follows an exponential path as more businesses adopt B2C tools. Again, the simulation results show that the upside of digital technology adoption is higher in Sub-Saharan Africa than in the Middle East and North Africa because the starting point is lower (as of 2017). The gains for Sub-Saharan Africa reach a plateau of about 90 percent higher in 2047 than in 2017, while the gains for the Middle East and North Africa are about 70 percent relative to 2017. Still, the maximum gains are reached, according to the simulations, only after about 20 years.

Conventional wisdom suggests that an increase in tourist arrivals is associated with an increase in jobs in the hospitality sector. Thus, Lopez-Cordova (2020) shows correlations between employment outcomes and tourist arrivals. Using those correlations, it is possible to speculate about the potential jobs that would be created if the scenarios depicted in figure 5.6 materialized. Figure 5.7 shows the results. Again, due to its lower starting point, the upside is higher for Sub-Saharan Africa than for the Middle East and

FIGURE 5.6   **Estimated Gains in Tourist Arrivals due to the Adoption of B2C Tools in the Middle East and North Africa and in Sub-Saharan Africa, 2017–47**

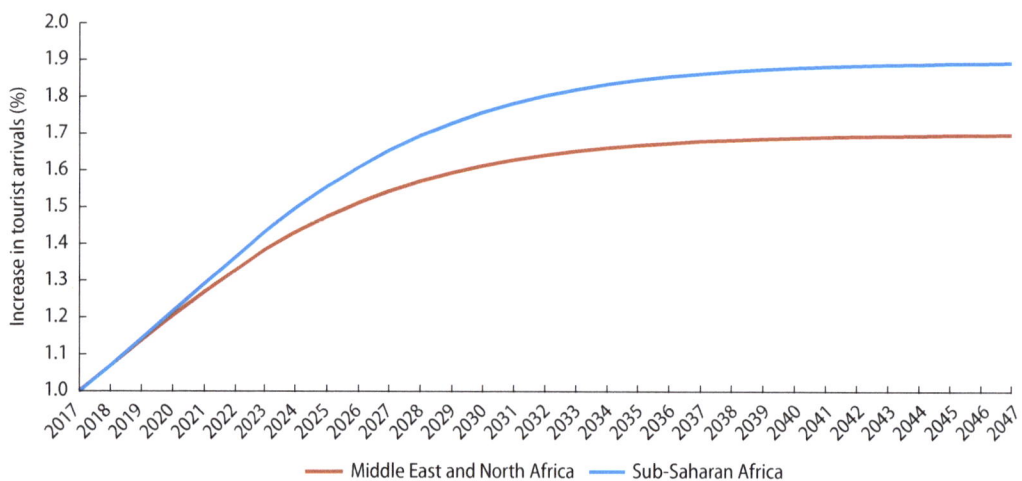

Source: Calculations based on results presented in Lopez-Cordova 2020.
Note: These scenarios correspond to the "high" scenario reported in Lopez-Cordova (2020). The adoption schedule for B2C digital tools follows the logit functional form discussed in the text. It is a faster adoption schedule than the concave function, which is more appropriate for modeling the spread of digital infrastructure than pure technology adoption. Lopez-Cordova (2020) estimates the elasticity of hospitality jobs with respect to tourist arrivals at slightly below 0.6%. The data for each region have been normalized to obtain start values of "1" in 2017. B2C = business-to-consumer.

FIGURE 5.7 **Estimated Gains in Tourism-Related Employment due to B2C Digital Technology Adoption in the Middle East and North Africa and in Sub-Saharan Africa, 2017–47**

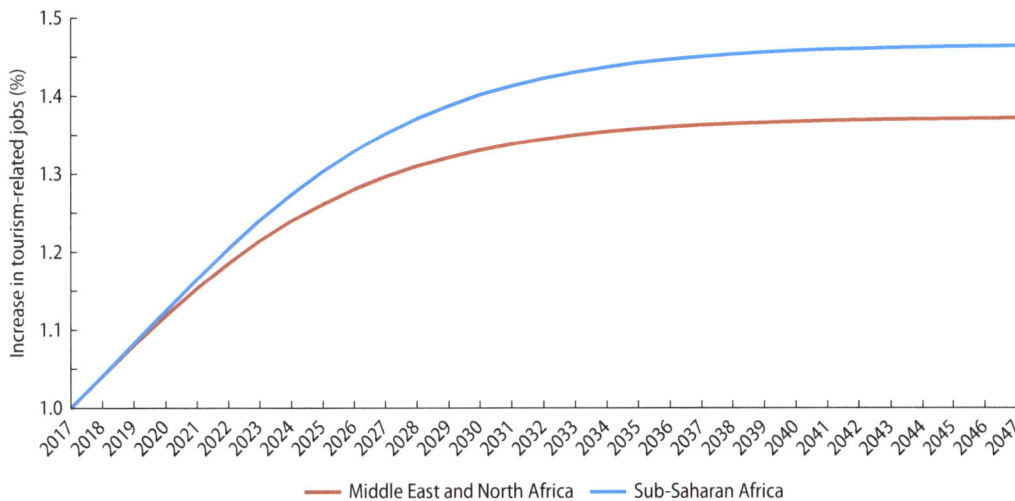

Source: Calculations based on results presented in Lopez-Cordova 2020.
Note: These scenarios correspond to the "high" scenario reported in Lopez-Cordova (2020). The adoption schedule for B2C digital tools follows the logit functional form. It is a faster adoption schedule than the concave function, which is more appropriate for modeling the spread of digital infrastructure than pure technology adoption. The data for each region have been normalized to obtain start values of "1" in 2017. B2C = business-to-consumer.

North Africa. The indicative gains in employment are roughly 46 percent in Sub-Saharan Africa and about 37 percent in the Middle East and North Africa. Due to the fast speed of B2C adoption, these gains are realized by 2034–35, after which gains plateau as countries reach the maximum potential B2C scores. If valid, these results imply large gains in employment when tourism and hospitality industries gain access to potential customers who speak different languages and come from farther away countries.

Reductions in Unemployment and Increases in Female Labor Force Participation

Digital technologies, including digital platforms, can also improve labor market outcomes by reducing search-and-matching costs between employers and job seekers, and increasing the quality and speed of matches between employers and workers. New research by Lederman and Zouaidi (2020) links the adoption of digital technologies to lower "frictional unemployment," which is the portion of unemployment that is not due

to the business cycle. More specifically, Lederman and Zouaidi estimate partial correlations between the use of the internet both in general and to make payments, on the one hand, and long-term unemployment, on the other hand. They find that only the incidence of digital payments (the percentage of adults who report using the internet to make payments in 2014 and 2017) is a robust predictor of frictional unemployment. Furthermore, estimates of the partial correlation tend to be slightly higher using instrumental variables rather than ordinary least squares, suggesting that the relationship is causal, whereby increases in the use of digital payments (but not internet use per se) lead to reductions in long-term unemployment rates.

Figure 5.8 presents the simulation results for the potential reduction in unemployment implied by the estimated marginal effects from Lederman and Zouaidi (2020) combined with a concave adoption schedule for digital payments. The graph plots the average (population-weighted) regional unemployment rates as use of the internet to make payments spreads across the adult population until it reaches 100 percent. The initial

FIGURE 5.8   **Decline in Unemployment due to the Diffusion of Digital Payments in the Middle East and North Africa and in Sub-Saharan Africa, 2017–33**

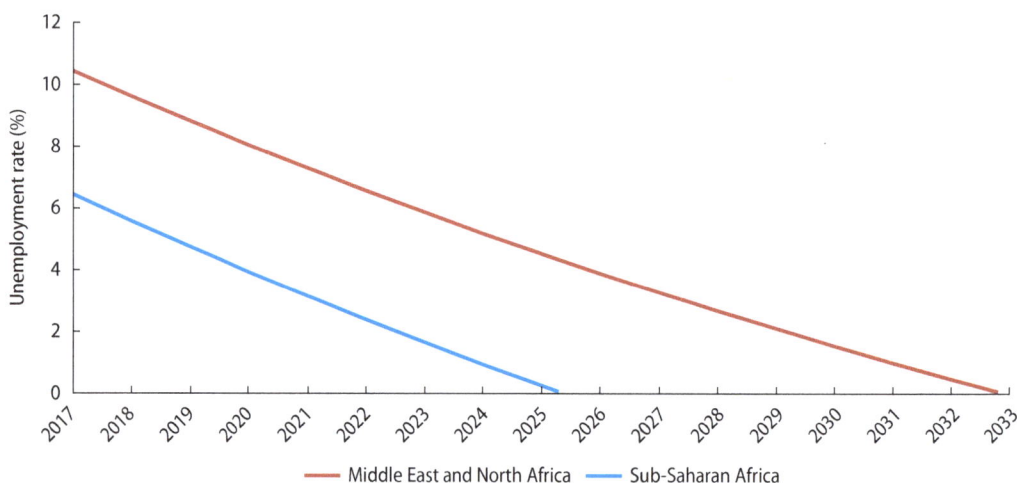

Sources: Calculations based on estimates by Lederman and Zouaidi 2020 and unemployment data from the International Labour Organization.
Note: The graph shows how long-run unemployment rates would fall for Sub-Saharan Africa and the Middle East and North Africa, on average (weighted by population), as digital payments (defined as using the internet to make a payment) approach 100% of the adult population. Unemployment rates are unlikely to become zero. As they decline, it is likely that labor markets will adjust through other margins, including reductions in informality and increases in real wages. The estimations by Lederman and Zouaidi (2020) control for cyclical factors as well as informality.

unemployment rate in 2017 was significantly lower in Sub-Saharan Africa than in the Middle East and North Africa, according to International Labour Organization statistics. Slowly but surely, the long-term unemployment rate declines. The graph shows a simulation with zero frictional unemployment that is unlikely to be realized because, as unemployment declines over time, labor markets are likely to adjust via other margins, including declines in informal employment and eventually higher real wages. These simulations assume that those variables remain unchanged. In other words, Lederman and Zouaidi (2020) control for those variables, producing estimates of the marginal effect of the incidence of digital payments that are inconsistent with labor market adjustments through multiple margins. In any case, the evidence is consistent with important impacts on unemployment that might be reflected through other variables.

Thus far, the evidence presented comes from international comparisons. However, recent research on the relationship between the advent of the internet and labor market outcomes is based on micro panel data from labor force surveys. El-Mallakh (2020) finds

that an internet job search in the Arab Republic of Egypt increases the chance of employment by 10 percentage points for an unemployed individual. However, this effect does not hold when considering only women or only rural job seekers. Labor force participation for women also is found to increase in Egypt with the use of job search platforms. In addition, Viollaz and Winkler (2020) find that the advent of internet connections via cell towers improved female labor force participation in Jordan. More specifically, a 1 percentage point increase in internet access led to an increase in female labor force participation of 0.8 percentage point, possibly owing to changing social norms.

However, cross-country evidence is consistent with the idea that the advent of the digital economy is associated with an increase in female labor force participation (FLFP). Lederman and Zouaidi (2020) estimate regression models linking FLFP across countries with the incidence of digital payments. The partial correlation is approximately +0.38, after controlling for women's education, GDP per capita as a proxy for wage levels, and inflation as a control for the business cycle (but the latter is not significant).

Figure 5.9 depicts these results. Similar estimates for male labor force participation are not statistically significant, implying that the digital economy might have a pro-female bias when it comes to labor force participation. This finding is consistent with the findings for Jordan reported by Viollaz and Winkler (2020).

Figure 5.10 shows the potential evolution of the regional FLFP for the Middle East and North Africa and Sub-Saharan Africa. It combines the marginal effect estimated

FIGURE 5.9   Correlation between Digital Payments and Female Labor Force Participation, 2017

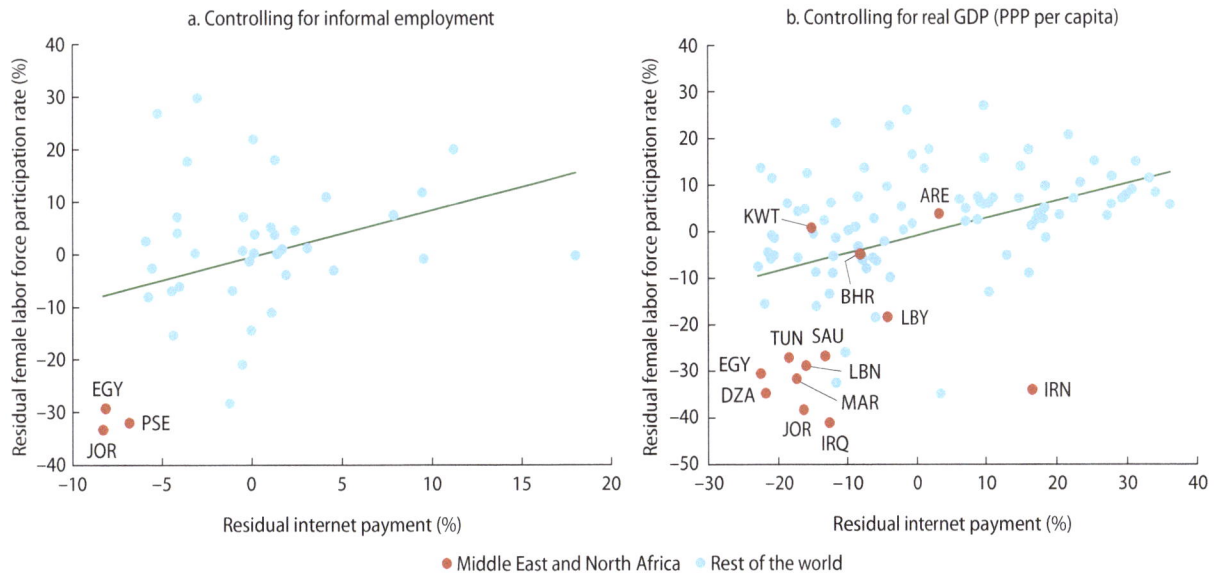

Sources: Calculations based on data from the Global Findex database, International Labour Organization ILO Stat database, and IMF 2020.
Note: Internet payments refer to "Used the internet to pay bills or to buy something online in the past year (% age 15+)." Panel a shows the correlation between internet payment and female labor force participation across countries in 2017, after controlling for informal employment. Panel b shows the correlation between internet payment and female labor force participation across countries in 2017, after controlling for real GDP PPP per capita. PPP = purchasing power parity.

FIGURE 5.10   Potential Increase in Female Labor Force Participation Rates from the Diffusion of Digital Payments in the Middle East and North Africa and in Sub-Saharan Africa, 2017–49

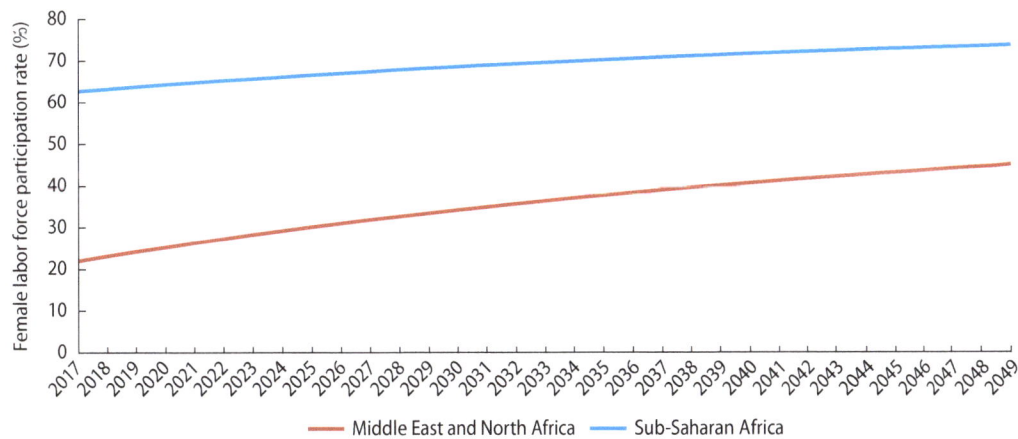

Sources: Calculations based on data from the International Labour Organization, the Global Findex database (Demirgüç-Kunt et al. 2018), and World Development Indicators.
Note: The estimated partial correlation between the incidence of digital payments and FLFP across countries used for these simulations is +0.38. The estimations control for learning-adjusted years of education of women in each country, informality, GDP per capita (PPP adjusted), and inflation rates (as a control of the business cycle). This estimate is from an ordinary least squares estimation, and it should be interpreted with care, because it does not necessarily indicate a causal effect of digital payments on FLFP. Estimates of the partial correlation between digital payments and male labor force participation are not statistically different from zero. FLFP = female labor force participation. PPP = purchasing power parity.

econometrically from international data with a concave function for the diffusion of digital payments across the adult population of each country. As of 2017, the FLFP rate was notably higher in Sub-Saharan Africa than in the Middle East and North Africa. But in both cases, by construction, the spread of digital payments tends to increase FLFP in the long run. Presumably, if the use of digital payments were to spread faster than in the business-as-usual scenario modeled in figure 5.10, the gains could be achieved sooner. For the Middle East and North Africa, the FLFP would almost double, from about 23 percent to more than 45 percent.

Summary of the Upside Impact of Digital Technologies

The analysis thus far has focused on the socioeconomic upsides for the digital economy. They appear to be large. GDP per capita could rise by more than 40 percent when digital infrastructure services approach universal coverage in the low- and middle-income economies of the Middle East and North Africa. Manufacturing productivity could rise by double digits when all formal manufacturing enterprises adopt business websites, and jobs in the sector could increase significantly. Furthermore, both results could occur relatively quickly if the digitalization of enterprises targets low-productivity firms first. Tourist arrivals could increase by 70 percent when the Middle East and North Africa reaches the maximum possible B2C scores, creating a significant number of jobs. Frictional unemployment could be virtually eliminated when all adults have adopted digital payments, and FLFP would almost double. So, the upside is high, and, as expected, the gains would occur across the economy. The issue, however, is how fast the region's population can achieve universal coverage. Chapter 6 discusses the implications for achieving these goals in three foundational pillars of the digital economy: infrastructure, digital payments, and regulations that shape the dynamism of e-commerce.

Notes

1. Calderon et al. (2019) present estimates indicating that countries with higher human capital (proxied by the log of the gross secondary education enrollment rate) tend to have higher marginal effects of increases in coverage of digital services than countries with lower levels of education. Figure 5.2 uses a common, relatively low estimate of the marginal effect: 0.412. In principle, because Sub-Saharan Africa has a lower secondary enrollment rate than the Middle East and North Africa (excluding the region's high-income countries), the marginal effect could be lower, and thus the upside depicted for Sub-Saharan Africa would also be lower. However, the estimates in Calderon et al. (2019) indicate that the interaction effect between education and digital infrastructure coverage is tiny with respect to the magnitude of the marginal effects. The computations of these differences are available from the authors on request.

2. Estimating the costs per user of offering digital infrastructure services is beyond the scope of this report. See Ellershaw et al. (2009) for a detailed assessment of the costs of serving rural communities in Australia. The differences across different types of digital network infrastructure are not that large due to the dominance in the use of physical cables across technologies. In principle, it is plausible that costs per user in low-density areas can be lowered by the use of newer technologies such as satellite internet. However, even in advanced economies, the coverage and quality (speed) of internet access in rural areas remains notably inferior to the services provided in urban areas (see, for example, Koeppel 2019).

3. The typical (median) enterprise in the estimation sample does not export, does not have a business website, and has a manager with 17 years of experience.

4. The assumed adoption rate is 5 percent. This rate corresponds to the average global annual adoption rate calculated using the last two waves of the World Bank Enterprise Survey panel data that Cusolito, Lederman, and Peña (2020) use to conduct their analysis.

5. For example, Brynjolfsson and Smith (2000) compare the prices of books and compact discs at online and offline retailers. They find that online prices are lower than offline

prices, although substantial price dispersion remains. Lower online prices have also been found in automotive products (Morton, Zettelmeyer, and Silva-Risso 2003) and airline fares (Orlov 2011). Persistence of dispersion is explained primarily by the intentional manipulation of search costs by firms. Retailers design their interfaces to make price search relatively difficult, lowering the price sensitivity of consumers and, thus, sustaining high margins for retailers (Ellison and Ellison 2009; Hossain and Morgan 2006).

6. Jensen (2007) examines the impact of mobile phone service on the fishing industry in the Indian state of Kerala, comparing prices for sardines in a variety of markets, before and after the arrival of mobile phone service. The findings show that the advent of mobile phones led to a sharp decline in price dispersion. Underlying the result is the rapid adoption of mobile phones coupled with the use of phones in fish markets. Aker (2010) also finds a similar result for grain markets in Niger, where mobile phone service is found to reduce price dispersion substantially. Moreover, Parker, Ramdas, and Savva (2016) examine a text message service in India, finding that the service reduced the price dispersion for crops.

7. The simulation results assume that the number of formal manufacturing enterprises in each country and region is fixed. That is, it assumes that there is no entry or exit of firms.

8. The estimates reported by Hjort and Poulsen (2019) are not strictly comparable to those in this report. Their study estimates the effect on employment in all sectors using labor force and other surveys of individuals. The estimates in figure 5.5 are for the formal manufacturing sector only, and the maximum gains are reached when all incumbent enterprises adopt a business website. To the extent that the adoption of a business website does not reach all existing enterprises, the total gains in employment would be smaller than those implied by the maximums reported in figure 5.5, panel a.

9. For a few cases, such as West Bank and Gaza and the Republic of Yemen, the indirect impact on labor demand is ignored because the surveys lack the data needed to compute revenue productivity. See Cusolito, Lederman, and Peña (2020) for technical details.

References

Aker, Jenny C. 2010. "Digitalization from Markets Near and Far: Mobile Phones and Agricultural Markets in Niger." *American Economic Journal: Applied Economics* 2 (3): 46–59.

Bresnahan, Timothy F., Erik Brynjolfsson, and Lorin M. Hitt. 2002. "Information Technology, Workplace Organization, and the Demand for Skilled Labor: Firm-Level Evidence." *Quarterly Journal of Economics* 117 (1): 339–76. https://doi.org/10.1162/00335 5302753399526.

Brynjolfsson, Erik, Wang Jin, and Kristina McElheran. 2020. "The Power of Prediction: Predictive Analytics, Organizational Complements, and Firm Performance." Working Paper, US Census Bureau, Suitland, MD.

Brynjolfsson, Erik, Daniel Rock, and Chad Syverson. 2017. "Artificial Intelligence and the Modern Productivity Paradox: A Clash of Expectations and Statistics." NBER Working Paper 24001, National Bureau of Economic Research, Cambridge, MA.

Brynjolfsson, Erik, and Michael D. Smith. 2000. "Frictionless Commerce? A Comparison of Internet and Conventional Retailers." *Management Science* 46 (4): 563–85.

Calderon, Cesar, Gerard Kambou, Vijdan Korman, Megumi Kubota, and Catalina Cantu Canales. 2019. "An Analysis of Issues Shaping Africa's Economic Future." *Africa's Pulse* 19, April 2019, World Bank, Washington, DC. https://openknowledge.worldbank.org/handle/10986/31499.

Comin, Diego, and M. Mestieri. 2013. "If Technology Has Arrived Everywhere, Why Has Income Diverged?" NBER Working Paper 19010, National Bureau of Economic Research, Cambridge, MA. http://www.nber.org/papers/w19010.

Comin, Diego, and Emilie Rovito. 2008. "An Exploration of Technology Diffusion." *American Economic Review* 100 (December): 2031–59.

Cusolito, Ana Paula, Daniel Lederman, and Jorge Peña. 2020. "The Effects of Digital-Technology Adoption on Productivity and Factor Demand: Firm-Level Evidence from Developing Countries." Policy Research Working Paper 9333, World Bank, Washington, DC. https://openknowledge.worldbank.org/handle/10986/34251.

De Loecker, Jan. 2019. "Digital Platforms and Productivity." Technical Note prepared for the Markets and Technology Unit, World Bank Group, Washington, DC.

Demirgüç-Kunt, Aslı, Leora Klapper, Dorothe Singer, Saniya Ansar, and Jake Hess. 2018. *The Global Findex Database 2017: Measuring Financial Inclusion and the Fintech Revolution.* Washington, DC: World Bank. https://www.worldbank.org/en/publication /gfdr/data/global-financial-development -database.

Ellershaw, John, Jennifer Riding, Alan Lee, An Tran, Lin Guan, Rod Tucker, Timothy Smith, and Erich Stumpf. 2009. "Deployment Costs of Rural Broadband Technologies." *Telecommunications Journal of Australia* 59 (2). doi: 10.2104/tja09029.

Ellison, Glenn, and Sara Fisher Ellison. 2009. "Search, Obfuscation, and Price Elasticities on the Internet." *Econometrica* 77 (2): 427–52.

El-Mallakh, Nelly. 2020. "Internet Job Search, Employment, and Wage Growth: Evidence from the Arab Republic of Egypt." Policy Research Working Paper 9196, World Bank, Washington, DC. https://openknowledge .worldbank.org/handle/10986/33518.

Goldfarb, Avi. 2020. "Digital Economics, Development, and the Rise of Platforms." Mimeo prepared for the World Bank Group, Washington, DC.

Goldfarb, Avi, and Catherine Tucker. 2019. "Digital Economics." *Journal of Economic Literature* 57 (1): 3–43.

Griliches, Zvi. 1957. "Hybrid Corn: An Exploration in the Economics of Technological Change." *Econometrica* 25 (4): 501–22.

Hjort, Jonas, and Jonas Poulsen. 2019. "The Arrival of Fast Internet and Employment in Africa." *American Economic Review* 109 (3): 1032–79.

Hossain, Tanjim, and John Morgan. 2006. ". . . Plus Shipping and Handling: Revenue (non) Equivalence in Field Experiments on eBay." *Advances in Economic Analysis and Policy* 5 (2): 1429.

IMF (International Monetary Fund). 2020. *World Economic Outlook: A Long and Difficult Ascent.* Washington, DC: IMF. October.

Jensen, Robert. 2007. "The Digital Provide: Information (Technology), Market Performance, and Welfare in the South Indian Fisheries Sector." *Quarterly Journal of Economics* 122 (3): 879–924.

Koeppel, Dan. 2019. "Moving to the Woods Killed My Internet. Here's What I Did about It." *Wirecutter* (blog), September 11, 2019. https://www.nytimes.com/wirecutter/blog /moving-to-the-wilderness-killed-my-internet/.

Lederman, Daniel, and Marwane Zouaidi. 2020. "The Incidence of Digital Economy and Frictional Unemployment: International Evidence." Policy Research Working Paper 9170, World Bank Group, Washington, DC. https://openknowledge.worldbank.org /handle/10986/33413.

Lopez-Cordova, Ernesto. 2020. "Digital Platforms and the Demand for International Tourism Services." Policy Research Working Paper 9147, World Bank, Washington, DC. https://openknowledge.worldbank.org/handle /10986/33352.

Morton, Fiona Scott, Florian Zettelmeyer, and Jorge Silva-Risso. 2003. "Consumer Information and Discrimination: Does the Internet Affect the Pricing of New Cars to Women and Minorities?" *Quantitative Marketing and Economics* 1 (1): 65–92.

Orlov, Eugene. 2011. "How Does the Internet Influence Price Dispersion? Evidence from the Airline Industry." *Journal of Industrial Economics* 59 (1): 21–37.

Parker, Chris, Kamalini Ramdas, and Nicos Savva. 2016. "Is IT Enough? Evidence from a Natural Experiment in India's Agriculture Markets." *Management Science* 62 (9): 2481–503.

Viollaz, Mariana, and Hernan Winkler. 2020. "Does the Internet Reduce Gender Gaps? The Case of Jordan." Policy Research Working Paper 9183, World Bank Group, Washington, DC. https://openknowledge.worldbank.org /handle/10986/33443.

World Bank. 2020. *World Development Report 2020: Trading for Development in the Age of Global Value Chains.* Washington, DC: World Bank. https://openknowledge.worldbank.org /handle/10986/32437.

World Bank. Various years. Global Financial Inclusion (Findex) (database). Washington, DC: World Bank.

World Bank. Various years. World Development Indicators (database). Washington, DC: World Bank.

Three Foundational Pillars of the Digital Economy | 6

As the framework of the report shows (chapter 3), creating an enabling environment is key for development of the digital economy. This chapter focuses on three essential pillars—digital infrastructure, digital payment system, and regulatory framework for e-commerce—underpinning the creation of an enabling digital environment and a well-functioning digital economy. The chapter explores the performance of countries in the Middle East and North Africa compared to other countries at similar levels of gross domestic product (GDP) per capita. While these pillars are necessary, they are by no means sufficient, as underscored by the region's digital paradox. As noted, the Middle East and North Africa significantly underperforms in digital payments, deviating by 15 percent from its predicted adoption level, conditional on the level of development. The lag in digital payments is not due to lagging information and communication technology (ICT) infrastructure and is apparently not due to banking sector constraints in and of themselves. Subject to data availability, further empirical analysis will shed further light on factors associated with the low adoption of digital payments in the region.

Digital Infrastructure

ICT infrastructure development varies across Middle East and North African countries and has scope to improve in absolute terms as regards coverage, quality, reliability, and affordability of internet services in many countries.[1] Further, fixed broadband coverage is below expectations relative to countries' GDP per capita. At the same time, however, the data indicate that, for the region's level of income per capita, network coverage is, on average, comparable to that of countries in other regions, mainly for 3G mobile networks for which there is at least 95 percent coverage (except for Djibouti and West Bank and Gaza). In terms of higher-capacity 4G networks, Middle East and North African countries (other than Djibouti and Iraq) are on par with their income group, with at least 75 percent coverage of the population, considered to be the minimum threshold for meaningful connectivity.[2] Some countries (mainly Gulf Cooperation Council members) have even higher-capacity 5G networks. With regard to internet costs for users, the Middle East and North Africa is within the average range for countries at similar income levels—on average, 1.7 percent of income per capita, which is less than the United Nations' affordability target of 2 percent of gross national income per capita (see figure B.6 in appendix B). Regarding internet speeds, outcomes are more dispersed in the Middle East and North Africa than in other countries at similar income levels (some countries overperform, while others underperform) (see figure B.5). Yet overall, infrastructure access does not explain the region's low development of digital payments adoption relative to other regions (see figures B.1 and B.3).

Digital Payments

Digital payment systems, which are essential for the digital economy to function, are also foundational for the emergence of other digital financial services, such as e-lending and e-savings. Notwithstanding the region's digital paradox, lags are also evident in traditional payment systems, which rely on access to bank accounts. Gévaudan and Lederman (2020) find that Middle East and North African countries have less well-developed payment systems than countries at similar levels of income. Irrespective of the type of payment (traditional or modern), countries, on average, appear below the fitted values, underperforming relative to other countries at similar income levels. Because this underperformance applies not only to digital payment methods but also to traditional payment systems, it is a sign that Middle East and North Africa lacks access to financial services sectorwide, begging the question why this is the case.

Arezki and Senbet (2020) note that the oversized role of the state in the economy is often thought to stifle private sector innovation and prevent advances in technology, ultimately hampering economic growth and employment creation. In the case of the banking sector in the Middle East and North Africa, at least, this does not seem to be borne out. Analysis conducted for this report assesses the effects of banking regulations and size of the banking sector on the incidence of digital payments.[3] The Middle East and North Africa is found to have the highest level of banking sector regulatory restrictions[4] (followed by East Asia and Pacific) and the second-largest banking sector in the world. The analysis examined the relationship between digital payments, bank regulations, and bank development to understand whether differences emerge in the effect of banking restrictions and banking system development on digital payments, stemming from varying the introduction (in the estimation model) of variables viewed as enablers of digital payments development.[5]

The analysis finds that, in all but one of the model specifications using all countries in the sample other than those in the Middle East and North Africa (rest of the world), restrictions on banking activities are statistically significant and negatively correlated with the development of digital payments. Likewise, in all but one specification using rest-of-the-world countries, banking system development (banking assets) is statistically significant, but in this case the relationship is positively correlated with the development of digital payments. For the three estimations in which the relationship is statistically significant, a 1 unit increase in the banking restrictions variable for the rest-of-the-world group of countries decreases the development of digital payments by a range of 1.8 to 2.9 percentage points; and a 1 unit increase in banking assets increases digital payments by a factor of 0.15 percentage point to 0.31 percentage point. Yet for the region, the reverse pattern is observed: more banking sector restrictions are associated with a higher incidence of digital payments (an effect of about 1 percentage point), while no correlation is found between size of the banking sector and incidence of digital payments (for details of the estimation model and results, see appendix A, table A.1). This result suggests that countries in the Middle East and North Africa have structural impediments to the development of digital payments that are not explained by the stringent regulations of the banking sector or by the development of the banking system.

Regulations for E-commerce

In the context of the digital economy, the regulatory environment is an enabler of digital technology adoption. It includes broad and diverse areas such as electronic transactions and signatures, consumer protection, antitrust, data protection, cybersecurity, and liability regulations. A more comprehensive regulatory environment can encourage the use of digital transactions by instilling greater trust in digital services. Based on a comparison of 20 countries in the Middle East and North Africa with 20 countries in other regions to measure the level of development of the enabling regulatory framework for e-commerce, middle-income countries (MICs) in the Middle East and North Africa are comparable with other MICs in the area of electronic documents but not in the areas of electronic signatures, data privacy protections, online consumer protections, and cybersecurity (figure 6.1, panel a). High-income countries (HICs) in the Middle East and North Africa, in contrast, compare well with other HICs in terms of electronic documents and e-signatures but lag other HICs with respect to all other regulatory areas (figure 6.1, panel b).

Countries in the Middle East and North Africa differ from countries in other regions, in that, despite an ICT infrastructure comparable to that of its peers (particularly mobile broadband), the region lags on an enabling regulatory environment for the digital economy and adoption of productive digital services such as mobile money. Regarding other indicators of the enabling environment, the Middle East and North Africa is on par with the world averages on e-government development (table B.4), yet slightly lags the world averages on the quality of institutions (table B.5).

The stringent regulations in the financial sector, however, do not seem to explain this underperformance. This effect is unique to the region, which further highlights the digital paradox. Nonetheless, Middle East and North African countries need not be relegated to slow growth of digital payments that progresses gradually and linearly through the different stages of payments. Gévaudan and Lederman (2020) find evidence suggesting the possibility of leapfrogging from a cash-based to a digital payment system, regardless of the level of banking system development. This leapfrogging could be achieved via growth in the use of mobile money, which does not necessarily depend on access to a traditional bank account. Kenya, which is less developed than countries in the Middle East and North Africa, shifted quickly to a level of noncash transactions via its mobile-based M-PESA system that now dwarfs Middle East and North African countries in terms of value of digital transactions.

FIGURE 6.1 **Benchmarking the Regulatory Framework for E-commerce, by Country Income Level**

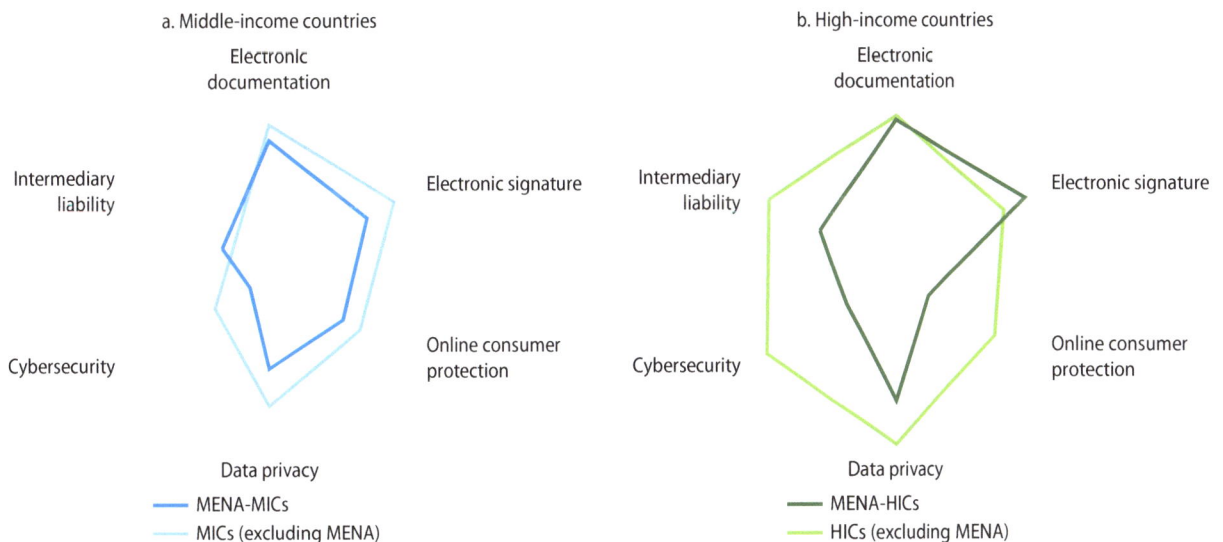

a. Middle-income countries

MENA-MICs
MICs (excluding MENA)

b. High-income countries

MENA-HICs
HICs (excluding MENA)

Source: Daza Jaller and Molinuevo 2020.
Note: HICs = high-income countries. MENA = Middle East and North Africa. MICs = middle-income countries.

A modernized regulatory framework or one that is flexible enough to adapt to new technologies, as was the case in Kenya, would help to build the trust needed to induce consumers to shift away from using cash.

While the foundational pillars are essential, the analog complements to digital economic growth and development—notably, contestability of markets, skills, and accountability—are equally essential, if not more so.

All this being said, the advent of digital technologies has raised issues in the public domain that go well beyond the potential upside in terms of socioeconomic gains. Chapter 7 discusses such challenges and risks.

Notes

1. Algeria has some of the lowest mobile speeds in the world, and Qatar and the United Arab Emirates have some of the fastest, likely reflecting the advent of 5G services.
2. See appendix B, figure B.1, panel d; figure B.3; and https://a4ai.org/meaningful-connectivity.
3. World Bank staff (Robert Cull, Daniel Lederman, and Davide Mare) compiled data on digital payments, banking regulations, and banking system development from the Findex survey (Demirgüç-Kunt et al. 2018), the Bank Regulation and Supervision Survey (World Bank 2019a), and the Global Financial Development Database (World Bank 2019b).
4. World Bank staff computed the degree of regulatory restrictions as an index that accounts for whether banks can participate in securities, insurance, and real estate financial activities.
5. The common enablers of digital payments introduced separately in the estimation model are secondary education enrollment, access to electricity, individuals using the internet, and mobile cellular subscriptions (see appendix A).

References

Arezki, Rabah, and Lemma W. Senbet. 2020. "Transforming Finance in the Middle East and North Africa." Policy Research Working Paper 9301, World Bank, Washington, DC. https:// openknowledge.worldbank.org/handle /10986/33996.

Daza Jaller, Lillyana Sophia, and Martín Molinuevo. 2020. "Digital Trade in MENA: Regulatory Readiness Assessment." Policy Research Working Paper 9199, World Bank, Washington, DC. https://openknowledge .worldbank.org/handle/10986/33521.

Demirgüç-Kunt, Aslı, Leora Klapper, Dorothe Singer, Saniya Ansar, and Jake Hess. 2018. *The Global Findex Database 2017: Measuring Financial Inclusion and the Fintech Revolution.* Washington, DC: World Bank. https://www .worldbank.org/en/publication/gfdr/data /global-financial-development-database.

Gévaudan, Clément, and Daniel Lederman. 2020. "Stages of Development of Payment Systems: Leapfrogging across Countries and MENA's Place in the World." Policy Research Working Paper 9104, World Bank, Washington, DC. https://openknowledge.worldbank.org /handle/10986/33153.

World Bank. 2019a. Bank Regulation and Supervision Survey (database). Washington, DC: World Bank. http://www.worldbank.org /en/research/brief/BRSS.

World Bank. 2019b. Global Financial Development Database. Washington, DC: World Bank. https://databank.worldbank.org /source/global-financial-development.

Addressing Challenges and Mitigating Risks | 7

The rise of digital technologies in the social and economic realms entails the accumulation of massive amounts of information and data, which poses challenges and risks stemming from how the data are accessed, safeguarded, processed, and deployed. Data generated from digital platforms and services have become a core asset fueling the creation of additional economic value and potentially spurring social interactions and activism. Data governance frameworks and market regulations can help to instill trust in digital information flows and mitigate risks posed by digital technologies such as anticompetitive practices by dominant firms, protection of individual privacy, and by spread of disinformation through social media. Concerns regarding competition extend to the information and communication technology (ICT) infrastructure markets in addition to the digital services subsector. This chapter examines these two concerns in turn, followed by a discussion of potential risks associated with social media. A penultimate section addresses the issue of data governance. A final section discusses data privacy in managing the COVID-19 pandemic.

Liberalization and Competition as Drivers of Mobile Digital Data Technology Adoption

The prospects for growth of the digital economy are inextricably linked with development of the ICT sector, even though the latter is not a sufficient enabler of the former.[1] Of particular relevance is the ICT sector's ability to acquire and deploy the latest technologies, which can favorably affect the price, quality, and coverage of digital services offered via broadband and mobile telephony. Technology adoption is a firm-level decision, influenced significantly by industry and market factors, but also by government policies, regulations, and actions, whether benevolent or captured by specific interests.

Much of the literature has focused on the evolution of regulations and competition policy after liberalization (see, for instance, Laffont, Rey, and Tirole 1997). Some studies, such as Cramton et al. (2011) or Rey and Salant (2012), assess how best to design procedures for allocating spectrum, which are common in liberalized mobile telecommunications markets, to guarantee downstream competition among operators. Other studies assess the role of independent regulatory bodies on telecommunications performance after privatization and find few benefits. Faccio and Zingales (2017) establish the positive effect of following regulatory best practices, as measured by the International Telecommunication Union (ITU) regulatory score, on various measures of market efficiency. They then question why countries do not systematically follow regulatory best practices and provide results supporting the regulatory capture theory.

Comin and Hobijn (2009) study the effect of institutional variables that affect the cost of lobbying and erecting barriers to entry on the speed of technology diffusion. Cervellati, Naghavi, and Toubal (2018) use the CHAT database (Comin and Hobijn 2009) to analyze the links between democratization, openness to trade, and incentives for technology adoption. But few empirical studies focus on the mobile telecommunications sector.[2]

A new study by Arezki et al. (2021) appears to be the first to exploit the sequenced launching of mobile telecommunications generations (1G to 5G) to explore the role of liberalization and independent regulatory agencies on the adoption of technology in the ICT sector. The study draws on several databases to construct four ICT sector indicators—technology adoption, liberalization, foreign participation, and regulatory independence (see appendix C for information on the construction of these indicators).

Figure 7.1 shows the evolution of the ranking for adoption of mobile telephony standards in the Middle East and North Africa and Sub-Saharan Africa. In contrast with North America, which jumped quickly to top rank and stayed there, some regions have progressed much more slowly up the technology ladder, while others have had swings in trajectory like the Middle East and North Africa, which has suffered a decline in ranking since 2008. Sub-Saharan Africa's ranking declined through 2006 but has since been improving (figure 7.1).

On the regulatory side, figure 7.2 shows that the share of countries with an independent regulatory authority is lower in the Middle East and North Africa than in other middle-income countries and Sub-Saharan Africa. Whether this gap handicaps the region's ability to bring about the adoption of the latest mobile telephony technologies is an empirical question, which is complicated by the fact that foreign entry into the mobile telephony market could be an alternative route for accelerating the pace of adoption.

Figure 7.3 shows the increasing liberalization of the telecommunications sectors in the Middle East and North Africa and Sub-Saharan Africa, while figure 7.4 shows the corresponding upward trend in foreign participation in the sector since 2000. These regions have among the highest levels of foreign participation in the world. Liberalization of the telecommunications sector, in the sense of allowing foreign direct investment and participation in the sector, might not be enough to help the region and other low- and middle-income countries to gain access to the latest generations of mobile telephony.

Arezki et al. (2021) explore the determinants of technology adoption, providing a view of how foreign entry and domestic regulatory independence interact to create the incentives for market participants to make the investments needed to provide customers with access to the latest generations of mobile telephony. Specifically, the study finds that liberalization and regulatory independence together (not separately) increase the rate of mobile technology adoption. Liberalization on its own is not sufficient to spur technology adoption; neither is foreign participation or regulatory independence on their own.

Table 7.1 presents a selection of econometric estimations linking competition to

FIGURE 7.1   **Mobile Technology Adoption Rankings in the Middle East and North Africa and in Sub-Saharan Africa, 1981–2019**

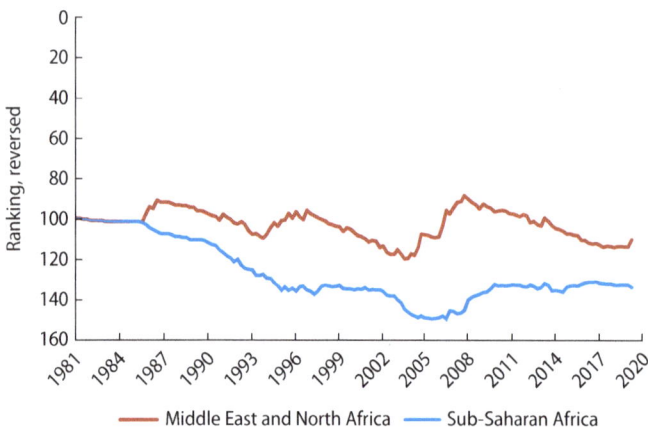

Source: Arezki et al. 2021.
Note: Country groups are represented by simple average rankings from all member countries for each specific year. For more details on technology adoption ranking, see Arezki et al. (2021).

technology adoption via liberalization and regulation. The table shows the importance of liberalization and independence of the telecommunications regulatory authority, combined, for increasing the rate of telecommunications technology adoption.[3] The variables used are described in appendix C. On their own, neither liberalization nor regulatory independence has coefficients that are statistically significant, nor are they robust across different model specifications. However, the coefficient associated with the interaction of liberalization and regulatory independence is statistically significant, across different regression specifications.[4] For example, the interaction coefficient of 9.9 in column (2) of table 7.1 indicates that an improvement in regulatory score by 0.3 can boost technology adoption by 3—that is, surpassing three countries in the ranking of mobile data technology adoption. Using foreign participation in the telecommunications sector (de facto liberalization), instead of de jure liberalization, yields the same result: the interaction coefficient of de facto liberalization with regulatory independence is positive (in this case with higher magnitudes) and statistically significant. In a nutshell, both liberalization and regulatory independence might be needed to help an economy to accelerate the pace of digital technology adoption. At least this seems to be the case for mobile data transmission technologies.[5]

Competition in the Digital Services Market

Issues relating to competition also arise in the digital services market, in the form of *anticompetitive practices*. The challenge emanates from the way in which data can be processed and used. With the rise of data-driven business models, decisions of governments and firms can be delegated to autonomous and self-learning algorithms, capable of processing information much more effectively than humans can, in many sectors ranging from automated stock trading to online retail pricing or in more day-to-day uses such as searching, gaming, or driving. These wide-ranging systems pose new types of challenges to antitrust laws and competition, including some that current policies

FIGURE 7.2   ICT Regulatory Authority Independence Index in the Middle East and North Africa and in Sub-Saharan Africa and by Country Income Group, 2017

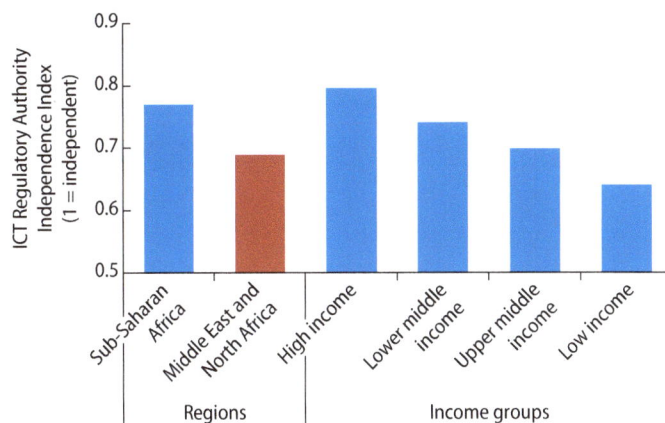

Source: Arezki et al. 2021, based on International Telecommunication Union data and World Bank calculations.
Note: Bars represent independence of the ICT regulatory authority. Scores are normalized to range between 0 and 1. Country groups are represented by the simple average of all member countries. ICT = information and communication technology.

FIGURE 7.3   Share of Liberalized Countries in the Middle East and North Africa and in Sub-Saharan Africa, 2000–18

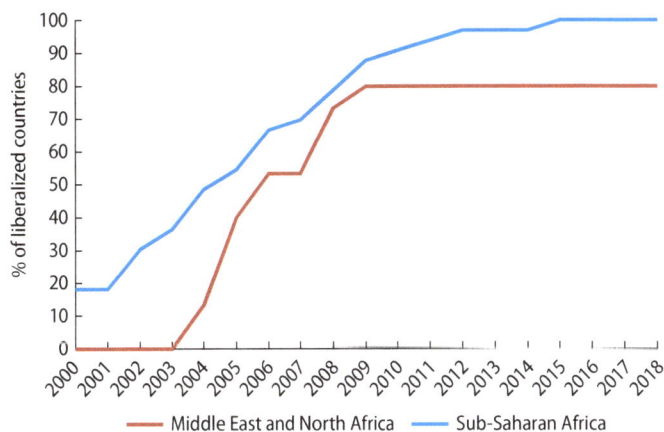

Source: World Bank staff calculations based on Telegeography data.
Note: Lines display the share of countries that have liberalized ICT. For more details on the liberalization of telecommunications, see Arezki et al. (2021). ICT = information and communication technology.

are not sufficiently geared to address. Governments around the world are undertaking specific reflections to tackle the challenges of digital competition and to understand how and why digital competition differs from traditional anticompetitive behavior (see COFECE 2018; Competition Bureau Canada 2017).

The availability of increasing amounts of personal information allows for more targeted price discrimination by digital

FIGURE 7.4   Share of Foreign Participation in the Middle East and North Africa and in Sub-Saharan Africa, 2000–18

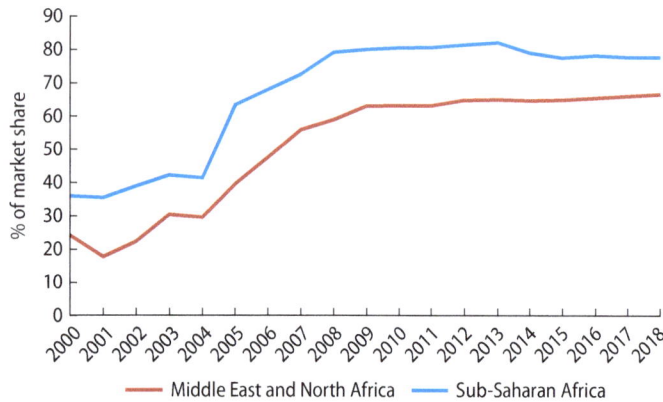

Source: Arezki et al. 2021.
Note: Regions are represented by the simple average of the foreign participation rate in their member countries. For more details on the foreign participation rate, see Arezki et al. (2021).

businesses. Such practices have ambiguous welfare implications. On the one hand, they can enhance efficiency when they lead to market contestability and increased consumer choices (for example, through more refined personalization of products). On the other hand, they can facilitate anticompetitive conduct or favor firms instead of consumers when firms charge different prices to key consumers to snare them from rival firms, thus thwarting the latter from achieving efficient scale. Digital platforms have incentives to capture as much personal data as possible from their users, whether needed for the platform to function or for improvement of the service supplied. For example, ride-hailing apps can track users even when they are not traveling

TABLE 7.1   Technology Adoption, Liberalization, and Regulatory Independence

| | Technology adoption score | | | |
| | Liberalization | | Foreign participation | |
Dependent variable	(1)	(2)	(3)	(4)
Liberalization (t−1)	−1.272	−4.759		
	(4.129)	(3.680)		
Foreign participation (t−1)			−5.605	−7.856*
			(5.736)	(4.753)
Regulatory score (t−1)	−10.76	−10.02	−10.55	−15.37***
	(7.162)	(6.170)	(6.658)	(5.704)
Liberalization (t−1) × regulatory score (t−1)	15.98**	9.941*		
	(7.054)	(6.011)		
Foreign participation (t−1) × regulatory score (t−1)			24.42***	23.88***
			(8.101)	(6.682)
Population (log) and GDP per capita (log)	Yes	Yes	Yes	Yes
Country and year fixed effects	Yes	Yes	Yes	Yes
Technology generation fixed effects	No	Yes	No	Yes
Observations	2,283	2,283	2,598	2,598
R-squared	0.807	0.842	0.810	0.851

Source: Arezki et al. 2021.
Note: Columns (1) and (2) correspond to columns (3) and (4), respectively, of table 1 in Arezki et al. (2021). Columns (3) and (4) correspond to columns (3) and (4), respectively, of table 2 in Arezki et al. (2021). Coefficient estimates are from ordinary least squares regressions at the country-year level, based on annual data from 2004 to 2018. Robust standard errors are given in parentheses. The dependent variable is the technology adoption score, where a higher number means a better ranking for and faster adoption of technology. Liberalization is a dummy variable, measured as 0 before the year of liberalization and 1 on the year of liberalization and thereafter. Regulatory score is an indicator between 0 and 1, where 1 indicates the highest score for ICT regulatory authority. The main variable of interest in columns (1) and (2) is the regulatory score interacted with liberalization; in columns (3) and (4), it is the regulatory score interacted with foreign participation. Regressions in all columns include constants and control for both country and year fixed effects; columns (2) and (4) also control for the fixed effect of the generation of technology adopted. ICT = information and communication technology.
* $p < 0.1$ ** $p < 0.05$ *** $p < 0.01$

anywhere, potentially turning a ride-enhancing feature into a surveillance tool.

Calvano et al. (2020) and Ezrachi and Stucke (2017) highlight the negative impact on competition practices posed by various types of machine-learning algorithms and the potential collusion that can result from several algorithms adapting to each other. Such "human-hands-off" artificial intelligence collusion algorithms are often found to be profit maximizing, in addition to being highly sophisticated in punishing deviations from the desired price and guiding a return to collusion outcomes (Calvano et al. 2020).

In multisided digital platforms where products offered on one side are usually free (such as most advertising-financed models), quality, in addition to privacy protection, is an important aspect of nonprice competition. However, there is a risk that the market will provide inadequate privacy protection because consumers do not believe that they have control over their data (Stucke and Grunes 2016). In a 2019 survey by the Pew Research Center in the United States, more than 80 percent of respondents said that they feel they have very little or no control over the personal data collected about them by the government and private firms (Auxier and Rainie 2019). Imperfect information thus creates a "dysfunctional equilibrium" with a lack of privacy competition, as consumer demand for privacy rights is too low to create strong market incentives.

Risk Associated with Digital Social Media

A further concern is the potential for adverse social effects emanating from social media use. As regards *social unrest*, the evidence is complex. Social media is linked to increased social activism, with a caveat that it is merely a conduit for connecting people around an existing discontent. Fergusson and Molina (2019) are among the first authors to identify a causal effect of Facebook on a global scale, using a credible strategy to identify the number of protests at the national, subnational, and individual levels. They estimate that, since Facebook's launch in 2006, it has contributed to increasing the number of protests in the world by between 14 percent and 22 percent.[6] The increased use of Facebook,[7] when available, reduces the costs of collective action. The emergence of Clubhouse, a participatory podcast-type app, is giving voice to many whose freedom of expression via traditional media is curtailed (Yee and Fassihi 2021). Social media also appear to have spillover effects on collective action across borders, giving inspiration to like-minded people in other countries (Arezki et al. 2020).

As regards the use of digital media for purposes of *radicalization*, evidence suggests that social media do not play a direct role. Berger and Morgan (2015) find that ISIS was successful in using Twitter to spread its message, but use of Twitter did not directly affect the number of terror attacks. Abdel Jelil et al. (2018) disaggregate the ISIS data at the country-education level to find that aspiring Daesh recruits have more education than the average male in their country of origin. The study tests for unemployment as a first-order driver of radicalization and provides evidence that individual-level socioeconomic conditions drive participation in violent extremism. Higher unemployment rates have a causal effect toward radicalization, especially for countries located closer to the Syrian Arab Republic. In particular, the study finds that a 1 percentage point increase in the unemployment rate would lead, on average, to 42 additional Daesh recruits. The study is in line with the literature showing that providing work opportunities and a positive socioeconomic environment helps to reduce other forms of violence, but it is the first to establish this causal relationship for recruitment into international terrorism.

A risk of digital data, beyond the privacy and market collusion concerns discussed above, is *disinformation* enabled via media manipulation and deep-fake technology. The large-scale aggregation of personal data can be a threat to individuals' integrity as well as to public goods such as national security. For this reason, an emerging legal literature argues that data regulations can borrow concepts from environmental protection regulations and laws (for example, Ben-Shahar 2019)—the concept of "data pollution," which refers to negative externalities produced by excessive data sharing or by the lack of privacy of information that consumers often experience with digital products. Disinformation campaigns are a central tool deployed by terrorism networks or foreign adversaries to destabilize national processes and policy debates. Fake news is defined as articles that are intentionally and verifiably false, with the goal of misleading readers. The spread of fake news on social media has become an important concern, especially in times of elections.

Effron and Raj (2019) assess the moral condemnation of fake news and its downstream consequences (intended social media behavior) in an experimental context. The experiments highlight the relationship between moral judgments and social media behaviors, as moral condemnation of previously seen headlines correlates positively with stronger intentions to share the headlines and less inclination to block or unfollow the person who posted it. The psychological experiment shows that even when headlines are clearly labeled as false and after statistically accounting for personal judgments on the accuracy, likeability, or popularity of the headlines, participants are more prone to share false headlines on social media if they have seen them at least one time before. Although the magnitude of the effect is small, on the order of 5–6 percent, the effect may well be amplified across billions of active social media users who regularly encounter fake news. By weakening moral condemnation, repeatedly encountering disinformation could have meaningful real-world consequences that may contribute to its spread and further reduce the censure of people who spread it.

Data Governance

Data governance and regulations can help to mitigate the risks posed by digital technologies—anticompetitive practices by dominant firms, protection of individual privacy, and spread of disinformation through social media. Establishing effective regulatory and data governance frameworks for the digital economy will be key for managing the challenges associated with availability of, and access to, massive amounts of digital data. These frameworks will help to foster data

privacy, reduce antitrust market behaviors, and instill trust in digital information flows. World Bank (2021) provides more extensive discussion of these issues.

A common view is that users generally own their personal data and give up disclosure of this information in exchange for accessing a product or service from a digital provider. However, data are also the result of a joint production effort between users and digital service providers and cannot be treated as personal property, since the information does not truly belong to any of those creating it but instead to the group generating it. An alternative to "data ownership" or "data management," therefore, is "data stewardship." In this light, the digital provider (whether a public or a private entity) takes on the role of a steward of the user's data, entrusted with stewardship obligations regarding how the data are collected, processed, used, shared, stored, secured, and disposed of.

Data stewardship requires trust between users and providers, and thereby strengthens nonprice competition for data privacy as firms face more pressure to offer data protection or transparency measures. The stewardship status delineates rights that are enshrined in privacy laws, consumer protection, bank secrecy, and data security. Data stewardship principles must be spelled out in specific privacy regulations, which are typically based on transparency, accountability, interoperability, and ability of the consumer to see the data collected about them, dispute their accuracy, and control how the information is used or shared. Table 7.2 depicts data stewardship as one dimension of a data governance framework conceptualized as a 2-by-2 matrix, with data categorized as being private or public and, on the second dimension, as being "traditional" or "new." Examples of data types are indicated in each of the four cells of the matrix.

This framework is appealing because it allows the regulation of digital platforms to highlight trade-offs in the choices concerning data governance approaches, trade-offs between the gains from data sharing, and concerns over privacy and cybersecurity. Digital platforms create value, but they also

TABLE 7.2   Data Stewardship in a Data Governance Framework

	Data stewardship	
Types of data	*Public*	*Private*
Traditional	Census; household surveys; national accounts; enterprise surveys	Any survey conducted by private entities, including public opinion surveys deployed by private entities (for example, Gallup)
New	E-gov digital platforms; digital identification; face recognition from public cameras; public procurement data; voter data; criminal records	Just-in-time data from private digital platforms; social media behavior; purchasing history; pricing algorithms; machine learning data sets

Source: Original framework for this publication.

aggregate a large amount of personal information, which raises privacy concerns. For example, when a private entity produces data—traditional or new—the public may have an interest in regulating its use, such as when there are concerns about privacy. Yet there is a governance trade-off between allowing data sharing across private entities (which can bring about economic gains) and negative spillovers beyond privacy concerns, such as cybersecurity risks or disinformation. For this reason, an emerging legal literature argues that data regulations can borrow concepts from environmental protection regulations and laws (Ben-Shahar 2019). The concept of "data pollution" refers to negative externalities produced by excessive data sharing or by the lack of information privacy that consumers often experience with digital products. The large-scale aggregation of personal data can be both a threat to individuals' integrity and a public good such as national security.

In the public sector, civil registration and digital identification are two of the most important enablers of digital services, but they should be governed with relevant data protection laws and regulations to ensure that only a minimum amount of data is shared. The laws governing digital identification should give people the ability to select the data they want to disclose, with simple means to correct inaccurate data and to know what data are being held about them and who has access to the information. The World Bank Identity for Development (ID4D) Initiative identifies several challenges that can affect the development of digital identification systems, including risk of exclusion, security violations, vendor or technology

lock-in, weak civil registration systems, limited connectivity infrastructure, low literacy, low trust in government capacity and regulatory services, and insufficient national cybersecurity capacity (World Bank 2019).

Efforts are under way in several countries to establish or update their data governance frameworks. The Arab Republic of Egypt, for example, passed a law to adopt new data protection legislation to attract offshore data center businesses. Bahrain, Jordan, Lebanon, Morocco, Oman, Qatar, and Tunisia enacted or updated their data protection laws in 2018. Other countries in the region (for example, Saudi Arabia and the United Arab Emirates) have considered a more prudent approach characterized by sector-specific data protection directives. Implementation of such legal and regulatory frameworks remains a work in progress, and efforts to finalize and adopt those frameworks must continue in view of remaining regulatory gaps (Daza Jaller and Molinuevo 2020).

Data governance frameworks should avoid inward-facing approaches by taking account of the cross-border nature of digital technologies and digital data flows. Some positive foundational initiatives exist for a regional digital technology framework, such as the Arab Digital Economy Strategy that aims to establish common principles and alignment on legislative and technological infrastructure across the Arab League. Middle East and North African countries could build on these initiatives and draw inspiration from already developed data governance paradigms (see box 7.1 on paradigms in China, the European Union, Singapore, and the United States), with suitable adaptation for the regional context.

BOX 7.1   Four Main Data Governance Paradigms

Cybersecurity, artificial intelligence, and data are key components of all digital development projects. Fundamentally, legal frameworks are needed to protect privacy and allow for the redress of harm. In the highly diverse global landscape of data governance, several paradigms of personal data governance are now discernible (with some common elements), but no convergence to a global standard is expected in the foreseeable future. Four broad paradigms have emerged in different country contexts.

The *European* paradigm views data use as a liability and thus emphasizes protection of personal privacy rights. The European Union's General Data Protection Regulation (GDPR), effective since May 2018, shifts the burden for maintaining the privacy and security of personal data to digital service providers by charging costs and imposing penalties if data collectors or processors allow data to be misused, lost, or stolen. The GDPR also limits the amount of personal data that businesses can collect, requiring that the information be "limited to what is necessary in relation to the purposes for which they are processed" (principle of data minimization). This model gives regulators unprecedented ability to penalize data abuses and authority over data collectors and processors.

The *United States* paradigm emphasizes data as an asset and is a more market-centric approach that specifies limited rules for the collection and selling of digital data outside the health and banking spheres. Businesses are permitted to own the data they have invested in collecting, whether by observing internet browsing patterns or through a credit bureau. This ownership provides data collectors an asset with economic value, although this asset cannot be valued on firms' balance sheets. The US focus on market behavior to determine collection and use of data has fostered the growth of giant tech firms such as Google and Facebook but has also been criticized for its lack of regulation and shortsighted approach to competition and individual rights.

In *China,* the state has ultimate authority over the data produced by users. Through strict control of companies operating in China (every entity doing business in China is required to host its data locally) and closed-circuit data sharing of camera footage, identification checks, WiFi connections, and health, banking, and legal records, China's government now has artificial intelligence systems that can recognize anyone in the country in real time and can link that identification to other data about them. Data flows freely to and within government departments and is designed specifically to further the government's social, political, and economic objectives.

Singapore's paradigm revolves around the expectation of accountability of the entities that manage personal data (the "data controllers") to all the stakeholders (customers, regulators, suppliers, business partners). The regulatory framework extends beyond compliance obligations to attempt to instill a permanent sense of urgency in organizations that use personal data, via requirements outlined in a series of frameworks and guidelines emphasizing data security, risk-based data management, trusted data sharing, transparent and human-centric artificial intelligence decisions, and proactive response in case of data breach. Data collaborations among private and public entities holding "big data" are also fostered within sandbox environments in which data sets are anonymized, then pooled to be analyzed to gain novel insights that can be beneficial for either public policy or commercial interests. Once the analysis is complete, the pooled data set is destroyed. Companies assessed as being good data stewards (through in-depth external audit procedures, which include visits on the premises and interviews with employees) are awarded the "Data Protection Trustmark" seal.

Data Privacy in Managing the COVID-19 Pandemic

Addressing data privacy is critical for the effective deployment of digital technologies to manage the COVID-19 pandemic, whether it be for detecting cases, tracing contacts, enforcing quarantine measures, strengthening health systems, or rolling out social and financial support to households and businesses affected by the pandemic.

The COVID-19 Privacy Guidelines prepared by the Global System for Mobile Communications Association (GSMA) outlines a series of approaches to comply with the general principles and ethics of data collection. These principles include complying with all existing laws and ethical guidelines, maintaining transparency about the sharing of data with governments and agencies, prohibiting the reidentification of individuals based on aggregated data, and sharing metadata only based on valid legal grounds, including possibly the valid consent of concerned individuals. GSMA estimates that it is "absolutely necessary and proportional" for governments to provide a law that can achieve a "specified and legitimate aim" for data sharing, "consistent with internationally recognized privacy standards, human rights, and other relevant laws" (GSMA 2020). Table 7.3 presents information on Middle East and North African countries that have introduced legislation on data governance to protect data privacy.[8] Additional information may also be found in the World Bank Digital Government Readiness Assessments implemented in Lebanon, Tunisia, and West Bank and Gaza.[9]

The use of big data in strategies for COVID-19 prevention and recovery requires the voluntary adoption of technology (software or applications) by the population, enabling digital infrastructure that can support the increased bandwidth, as well as real-time information sharing between digital content providers and public authorities. Likewise, it requires trust from the public that the authorities will respect privacy laws and not abuse them now or in the future. It also requires transparent leadership to allow for responsible use of data and foster evidence-based assessments and policy making. While there are tremendous opportunities in the Middle East and North Africa to bolster the use of big data as a means to cope with the pandemic, Arezki et al. (2020) note that the lack of transparency on data governance may severely affect the successful and sustainable realization of these approaches.

TABLE 7.3   Regulation on Data Privacy in the Middle East and North Africa

Country	Sensitive data Special treatment	Legal bases for data collection and processing				Data subjects' rights Access or deletion	Cross-border data transfers	
		Consent	Performance of a contract	Legal obligation	Legitimate interests		Rules on transfers	No data localization
Algeria	•	•	•	•	•	•	•	•
Bahrain	•	•	•	•	•	•	•	•
Iran, Islamic Rep.	•	•				•		•
Israel	•	•				•	•	•
Kuwait		•				•		•
Lebanon	•					•		•
Morocco	•	•	•	•	•	•	•	•
Oman		•		•		•	•	•
Qatar	•	•		•	•	•		•
Saudi Arabia		•		•				•
Tunisia	•	•	•			•	•	•
United Arab Emirates		•					•	•

Source: Daza Jaller and Molinuevo 2020.

Notes

1. This section relies heavily on Arezki et al. (2021).

2. Wallsten (2001) focuses on Latin American and African countries for the period 1984–97, establishing that competition is associated with lower prices and better access. Ezzat and Aboushady (2018) study the sequencing of reforms in Middle East and North African countries, showing that creating an independent regulator before privatizing the incumbent facilitates the entry of competitors.

3. See Arezki et al. (2021, app. table 3) for the list of countries used in the regressions in table 7.1.

4. Both regressions control for country fixed effects, the logarithm of population, and the logarithm of gross domestic product (GDP) per capita. Column (1) also controls for year fixed effects, while column (2) adds controls for the fixed effect of the generation of the standard adopted. Other specifications included in Arezki et al. (2021) also show interaction coefficients that are statistically significant.

5. There is a subtle difference between the "coverage" of digital infrastructure services (such as access to the internet) and "digital technology adoption" (such as use of the internet to make digital payments or, in this case, adoption of the latest generation of mobile data transmission technology). These differences are subtle because of the practical overlap between service coverage and technology adoption—the latter can only occur when enterprises or individuals have access to digital telecommunications services that require building infrastructure. The case of mobile data transmission technologies includes elements of both concepts, because the adoption of a given generation of technologies—for example, 5G—requires some investments in physical infrastructure. But moving from 3G to 4G might require minimum investments such as retrofitting existing infrastructure.

6. This effect is sizable; it is estimated by measuring the introduction of Facebook in local languages and its impact on the number of protests every month after controlling for several relevant socioeconomic characteristics. Fergusson and Molina (2019) base their analysis on the number of "Facebook speakers," the share of each country's population who can access a version of Facebook in their native language. The measure of protests comes from the Global Database of Events, Language, and Tone, a global and daily database recording different types of collective action events (GDELT Project, various years).

7. As Facebook does not publicly disclose the number of users at the country-month level, Fergusson and Molina (2019) use search interest for Facebook in Google Trends as a proxy for the use of Facebook.

8. In a state of emergency, special rules may waive some of these restrictions on data protection.

9. Although the full results of these assessments may not yet be publicly disclosed, information on the assessments can be found in World Bank (2020).

References

Abdel Jelil, Mohamed, Kartika Bhatia, Anne Brockmeyer, Quy-Toan Do, and Clement Joubert. 2018. "Unemployment and Violent Extremism: Evidence from Daesh Foreign Recruits." Policy Research Working Paper 8381, World Bank, Washington, DC. https://openknowledge.worldbank.org/handle/10986/29561.

Arezki, Rabah, Alou Adesse Dama, Simeon Djankov, and Ha Nguyen. 2020. "Contagious Protests." Policy Research Working Paper 9321, World Bank, Washington, DC. https://openknowledge.worldbank.org/handle/10986/34130.

Arezki, Rabah, Vianney Dequiedt, Rachel Yuting Fan, and Carlo Maria Rossotto. 2021. "Liberalization, Technology Adoption, and Stock Returns: Evidence from Telecom." Policy Research Working Paper 9561, World Bank, Washington, DC. https://openknowledge.worldbank.org/handle/10986/35210.

Auxier, Brooke, and Lee Rainie. 2019. "Key Takeaways on Americans' Views about Privacy, Surveillance, and Data-Sharing." *Fact Tank News in the Numbers* (blog), November 15, 2019. https://www.pewresearch.org/fact-tank/2019/11/15/key-takeaways-on-americans-views-about-privacy-surveillance-and-data-sharing/.

Ben-Shahar, Omri. 2019. "Data Pollution." *Journal of Legal Analysis* 11: 104–59.

Berger, J. M., and Jonathon Morgan. 2015. "ISIS Twitter Census: Defining and Describing the Population of ISIS Supporters on Twitter." Brookings Institution, Washington, DC.

Calvano, Emilio, Giacomo Calzolari, Vincezo Denicolò, and Sergio Pastorello. 2020.

"Artificial Intelligence, Algorithmic Pricing, and Collusion." *American Economic Review* 110 (10): 3267–97.

Cervellati, Matteo, Alireza Naghavi, and Farid Toubal. 2018. "Trade Liberalization, Democratization, and Technology Adoption." *Journal of Economic Growth* 23 (2): 145–73.

COFECE (Comisión Federal de Competencia Económica). 2018. "Rethinking Competition in the Digital Economy." COFECE, Mexico City.

Comin, Diego, and Bart Hobijn. 2009. "Lobbies and Technology Diffusion." *Review of Economics and Statistics* 91 (2): 229–44.

Competition Bureau Canada. 2017. "Big Data and Innovation: Implications for Competition Policy in Canada." Competition Bureau Canada, Gatineau.

Cramton, Peter, Evan Kwerel, Gregory Rosston, and Andrzej Skrzypacz. 2011. "Using Spectrum Auctions to Enhance Competition in Wireless Services." *Journal of Law & Economics* 54 (November): S167–S188.

Daza Jaller, Lillyana Sophia, and Martín Molinuevo. 2020. "Digital Trade in MENA: Regulatory Readiness Assessment." Policy Research Working Paper 9199, World Bank, Washington, DC. https://openknowledge .worldbank.org/handle/10986/33521.

Effron, Daniel A., and Medha Raj. 2019. "Misinformation and Morality: Encountering Fake-News Headlines Makes Them Seem Less Unethical to Publish and Share." *Psychological Science* 31 (1): 75–87.

Ezrachi, Ariel, and Maurice E. Stucke. 2017. "Artificial Intelligence and Collusion: When Computers Inhibit Competition." *University of Illinois Law Review* 2017 (5): 1775–809.

Ezzat, Riham Ahmed, and Nora Aboushady. 2018. "Do Restrictive Regulatory Policies Matter for Telecom Performance? Evidence from MENA Countries." *Utilities Policy* 53 (August): 60–72. https://doi.org/10.1016/j .jup.2018.05.003.

Faccio, Mara, and Luigi Zingales. 2017. "Political Determinants of Competition in the Mobile Telecommunication Industry." NBER Working Paper 23041, National Bureau of Economic Research, Cambridge, MA.

Fergusson, Leopoldo, and Carlos Molina. 2019. "Facebook Causes Protests." CEDE Working Paper 018002, Centro de Estudios sobre Desarrollo Económico, Universidad de los Andes, Bogotá, Colombia. https://repositorio .uniandes.edu.co/handle/1992/41105.

GDELT Project. Various years. Global Database of Events, Language, and Tone (database). https://catalog.data.gov/dataset/global -database-of-events-language-and-tone -gdelt-project.

GSMA (Global System for Mobile Communications Association). 2020. "COVID-19 Privacy Guidelines." *Public Policy* (blog), April 6, 2020. https://www .gsma.com/publicpolicy/resources/covid-19 -privacy-guidelines.

Laffont, Jean-Jacques, Patrick Rey, and Jean Tirole. 1997. "Competition between Telecommunications Operators." *European Economic Review* 41 (3-5): 701–11.

Rey, Patrick, and David Salant. 2012. "Abuse of Dominance and Licensing of Intellectual Property." *International Journal of Industrial Organization* 30 (6): 518–27.

Stucke, Maurice, and Allen P. Grunes. 2016. "Introduction: Big Data and Competition Policy." In *Big Data and Competition Policy.* Oxford, U.K.: Oxford University Press.

Wallsten, Scott J. 2001. "An Econometric Analysis of Telecom Competition, Privatization, and Regulation in Africa and Latin America." *Journal of Industrial Economics* 49 (1): 1–19.

World Bank. 2019. *ID4D Practitioner's Guide.* Version 1.0. Washington, DC: World Bank Group, ID4D (Identification for Development). http://documents.worldbank.org/curated /en/248371559325561562/ID4D-Practitioner -s-Guide.

World Bank. 2020. *Digital Government Readiness Assessment Toolkit: Guidelines for Task Teams.* Washington, DC: World Bank.

World Bank. 2021. *World Development Report 2021: Data for Better Lives.* Washington, DC: World Bank. https://openknowledge .worldbank.org/handle/10986/35218.

Yee, Vivian, and Farnaz Fassihi. 2021. "Clubhouse App Creates Space for Open Talk in Middle East." *New York Times,* May 2, 2021. https://www.nytimes.com/2021/05/02 /world/middleeast/clubhouse-iran-egypt -mideast.html (accessed May 2, 2021).

Summary and Conclusions

8

The report begins in chapter 1 by documenting a digital paradox in the Middle East and North Africa: the region has an excess of social media accounts for its level of development but exhibits glaring gaps in use of the internet to make payments. The evidence presented cannot fully account for this paradox, but it does yield several observations. The coverage of digital infrastructure services, particularly mobile broadband, is roughly on par with what is predicted by the region's level of gross domestic product (GDP) per capita, but the population's adoption of digital payments is low relative to its level of development. The reason for this glaring gap is subject to speculation, although circumstantial evidence suggests that lack of societal trust in government and the financial system are part of the explanation. Following the presentation of data on the region's digital paradox, chapter 2 discusses the correlations between indicators of trust, use of digital payments, and transparency. Chapter 3 proposes a logical framework in which trust not only is affected by regulatory policies such as laws that protect consumers and personal data privacy, but also helps to determine the population's level of adoption of digital tools, such as using the internet to pay bills.

The region's digital paradox notwithstanding, chapter 4 describes the key channel through which digital technologies can help to raise economic growth and create jobs—overcoming market barriers. It presents evidence of how transactions in digital platforms can provide information that helps to improve the quality of ride-hailing services. Recent research commissioned for this report indicates that the information technology sector in West Bank has helped to cushion the economic blow of mobility barriers. The chapter presents estimates, also commissioned for this report, about how the adoption of digital technology can help to reduce the economic costs of geographic distance and language barriers in the tourism industry.

After establishing the mechanisms through which digital technologies support economic activity, chapter 5 provides lower-bound estimates of the economic upside of a digital economy for the Middle East and North Africa compared to Sub-Saharan Africa. The evidence is nuanced, but overall approaching the aspirational goal of achieving universal coverage of digital infrastructure and universal adoption of digital tools by individuals and enterprises is likely to bring substantial gains in growth and jobs. The evidence here is nuanced as well. For example, universal digitalization of formal manufacturing enterprises in the Middle East and North Africa will possibly lead to lower corporate profits as the domestic prices of manufactured goods could fall. Thus, consumers will reap some of the economic benefits of the digital economy if competition increases.

The issue is how fast the gains from digital can accrue. The analysis finds that the largest gains occur by prioritizing access to underserved populations, enabling more rapid cumulative increases in economic gains. Expanding digital payments is key for digital transformation of the economy. Without it, the region's digital economy will remain nascent. For this reason, the report's finding of a digital paradox is concerning. The divergence in the use of digital technology for social versus economic purposes is unique to the Middle East and North Africa. That gap must be bridged to spur the region's digital economic transformation.

Chapter 6 explores three essential pillars underpinning a well-functioning digital economy—digital infrastructure, digital payments system, and regulatory framework for e-commerce—to assess the adoption (use) of digital technology in Middle East and North African countries compared to other countries at similar levels of GDP per capita. While the pillars are necessary for growth of the digital economy, they are by no means sufficient, as underscored by the region's digital paradox and levels of information and communication technology (ICT), which are largely comparable to those of other regions in terms of overall access, download speed, or costs of services, particularly regarding mobile broadband. The region's ICT constraints are likely linked to conditions in the telecom sector. The report presents analysis showing the importance of liberalization and contestability of the telecom sector, in addition to independence of the telecom regulatory authority, for increasing the rate of adoption of improved telecom technologies.

The lower-than-predicted levels of digital payment use are found not to be linked to banking sector constraints. For countries in other regions, a higher incidence of digital payments is found to be positively correlated with banking sector restrictions and size of the banking sector; yet the reverse pattern is observed in the Middle East and North Africa regarding banking sector restrictions, and no correlation is found regarding banking sector size. Impediments to the development of digital payments are not yet discernible empirically, but they seem to be linked to structural features of the banking sector rather than being the result of stringent regulations or level of development of the banking system.

The banking sector constraints likely lie in characteristics such as noncontestable markets and the large share of state-owned enterprises in the banking sector. Further review by financial and banking sector specialists is warranted to understand better the structural impediments in Middle East and North African countries and the promise of mobile money growth in the region. In parallel, opening up the region's telecom markets could expand the use of mobile money and digital payments, while pursuing financial inclusion via an increase in traditional bank accounts.

As regards the enabling regulatory framework for e-commerce (covering electronic transactions and signature, consumer protection, antitrust, data protection, cybersecurity, and liability regulations), limited evidence so far suggests that Middle East and North African countries have further work to do. The region's middle-income countries (MICs) are comparable to MICs in other regions except in the areas of electronic signature, data privacy protections, online consumer protections, and cybersecurity. In contrast, its high-income countries (HICs) compare well with other HICs in terms of electronic documents and e-signatures but lag with respect to all other regulatory areas. Whether lags in these factors constitute binding constraints to digital payments remains an open question to be explored further empirically, subject to data availability.

Lastly, the report discusses the implications of the emergence of massive amounts of social and economic digital data, and examines the challenges and risks stemming from how data are accessed, safeguarded, processed, and deployed. Digital data use must be guided by an effective data governance framework that instills trust in digital information flows and helps to mitigate the risks posed by digital technologies such as anti-competition practices by dominant firms, breaches of individual privacy protection, and spread of disinformation through social media.

In sum, the analyses in this report suggest that the Middle East and North Africa could prioritize the expansion of digital payments in addition to universal access to broadband. To reap the most rapid economic gains from digitalization, priority in access to digital broadband should be given to underserved populations, although the report does not examine the costs of bringing digital infrastructure services to underserved populations within countries. Existing evidence from high-income economies, such as Australia and the United States, indicates that reaching rural consumers can be more costly than reaching urban dwellers.

As discussed in chapter 7, enhanced openness and contestability of telecom and banking sectors, and updated sector regulations implemented independent of political influence, are likely needed to achieve the rapid expansion of digital payments. Furthermore, a more dynamic telecom sector could spur innovations in the development and use of mobile broadband services and mobile money accounts. In this regard, ensuring greater competition in telecom markets is important for achieving equitable access, quality, and affordability of broadband services.

Trust in the use of digital payments is a key issue, which could be enhanced via e-government mechanisms. Evidence so far suggests that e-government options—such as digital cash transfers, digitized payment mechanisms for public services, and a shift to e-procurement—offer great promise for facilitating the rapid expansion of digital money in a way that quickly builds a level of trust and comfort in the use of digital payments for commercial purposes. Further empirical analysis is needed to shed more light on the role of trust in the digital economy.

Appendix A: Modeling the Relationship between Digital Payments, Bank Regulation, and Banking System Development

The Empirical Modeling

To investigate the relationship between digital payments, bank regulation, and bank development, World Bank staff Robert Cull, Daniel Lederman, and Davide Mare estimated a pooled cross-sectional regression at the country level:

$$Digital\ payments_{it} = \alpha + \beta\ Banking\ Restrictions_{it} + \delta\ Banking\ Development_{it} + \gamma\ Other\ controls_{it} + \varepsilon_{it}, \tag{A.1}$$

where subscripts i and t stand for country and time, respectively, *Digital payments* is the percentage of respondents who report using the internet to pay bills or buy something online, *Banking Restrictions* is an index that captures the degree of stringency in the financial activities that banks may undertake, *Banking Development* is banks' assets as a share of gross domestic product (GDP), and *Other controls* is a set of variables that account for the macroeconomic environment and the enablers of digital payments development. The regressions also include a dummy variable that takes the value of 1 for 2014 and 0 otherwise. This dummy controls for the initial level of digital payments and any potential differences

that characterize the two years in the analysis (the other year being 2017). Robust standard errors were also computed to correct the error term for heteroskedasticity in the residuals.

The analysis explored whether the development of digital payments is associated with the degree of stringency in banking regulations and the level of development of the banking system. Equation A.1 was estimated four times, each one reflecting the introduction of a different control that represents an enabler of digital payments development. The analysis sought to understand whether, by varying the enablers of digital payments development, the β coefficients are still significant for inferring whether the banking restriction and banking size effects are driven by the enabler variable specified.

The Results

Table A.1 reports the results of the pooled cross-sectional estimations using equation A.1. In all but one specification using all countries in the sample other than the Middle East and North Africa (rest of the world), restrictions on banking activities are statistically significant and negatively associated with the development of digital payments.[1] Likewise, in all but one specification using the rest-of-the-world countries, banking system development (banks' assets) is statistically significant, but now the relationship is positively associated with the development of digital payments. For the regressions in which the relationship is statistically significant, a 1 unit increase in the banking restrictions variable decreases the development of digital payments by a range of 1.8 to 2.9 percentage points, and a 1 unit increase in banking assets increases digital payments by a factor of 0.15 to 0.31 percentage point.

Enabling factors were introduced separately in the estimations to lessen problems of multicollinearity. Results remain qualitatively the same, although in the specification with a control for percentage of the population using the internet (table A.1, column 3), the coefficients on the restrictions on banking activities and the level of banking development (banks' assets) for the rest of the world become statistically insignificant. This is not surprising, as the variable accounting for the presence of physical infrastructure (access to the internet) is strongly correlated with use of the internet

to make payments (correlation of 0.8). In contrast, the interaction terms of the banking variables with the Middle East and North Africa are significant for the "using the internet" specification, along with two other specifications, but fail to be significant in the specification relating to secondary education enrollment.

In summary, irrespective of the control of enablers used, both the banking restrictions coefficient and the banking assets coefficient for the Middle East and North Africa differ from those for the rest of the world. A reasonable conclusion is that the lower use of digital payments in the Middle East and North Africa does not stem from more stringent banking regulations or from banking system development. As such, an alternate explanation for the low use of digital payments in the Middle East and North Africa must be sought.

Table A.2 reports the name, description, and source of the variables included in the analysis.

TABLE A.1   Relationships between Banking Restrictions, Financial Development, and Digital Payments

Dependent variable: Used the internet to pay (% age 15+)

Independent variable	(1)	(2)	(3)	(4)
RoW restrictions on banking activities	−1.793*	−2.768***	−1.043	−2.903***
	(0.914)	(0.987)	(0.726)	(1.002)
MENA	−26.099*	−22.372	−24.686**	−15.618
	(14.165)	(17.117)	(9.925)	(17.834)
MENA × banking restrictions	3.003	3.979*	2.680*	4.075*
	(1.934)	(2.370)	(1.517)	(2.394)
RoW banks' assets (% of GDP)	0.150***	0.248***	0.062	0.310***
	(0.046)	(0.060)	(0.039)	(0.052)
MENA × banks' assets	−0.082	−0.285**	−0.150*	−0.344***
	(0.092)	(0.113)	(0.090)	(0.111)
Controls: Enablers of digital payments[a]				
Controls: Macroeconomic variables[b]		[...]		
Initial year dummy and constant[c]				
Observations	166	166	166	166
Adjusted *R*-squared	0.588	0.478	0.709	0.451

Sources: World Bank estimates, based on a pooled cross section of data from the World Bank Findex database, the Bank Regulation and Supervision Survey, the Global Financial Development Database, and the World Development Indicator database.

Note: Robust standard errors for heteroskedasticity appear in parentheses. For a description of the variables, see table A.2. Statistical significance is at the two-tailed level. MENA = Middle East and North Africa. RoW = rest of the world.

a. Columns (1) to (4) use different controls of common enablers of digital payments, respectively: (1) secondary education enrollment, (2) access to electricity, (3) individuals using the internet, and (4) mobile cellular subscriptions.

b. The regressions control for the macroeconomic environment (average growth of GDP per capita, population, and consumer price index inflation).

c. The regressions also include a dummy variable that takes the value of 1 for 2014 and 0 otherwise. This controls for the initial level of digital payments and any potential difference that characterizes the two years in the analysis (the other year being 2017).

*p < .10   **p < .05   ***p < .01

TABLE A.2   **Description of Variables**

Variable	Description	Source
Dependent variable		
Used the internet to pay (% age 15+)	The % of respondents who reported using the internet to pay bills or buy something online in the past 12 months	Global Findex
Independent variables		
Banking		
Overall restrictions on banking activities (three components)	Level of regulatory restrictions for bank participation in securities activities, insurance, and real estate financial activities	BRSS
Overall restrictions on banking activities—extended (four components)	Level of regulatory restrictions for bank participation in securities activities, insurance, real estate financial activities, and nonfinancial businesses; the question on nonfinancial businesses became available in the fourth round of the BRSS	BRSS
Restrictions on banks owning voting shares in nonfinancial firms	A categorical variable that takes the value of 1 for the least restrictive regulation and 4 for the most restrictive regulation	BRSS
Prohibition on the entry of foreign banks in the domestic banking market	A categorical variable that takes the value of 0 for the least restrictive regulation for foreign banks' entry into the domestic banking market and 4 for the most restrictive regulation	BRSS
Index for regulatory restrictions	Overall regulatory index for restrictions in the areas of securities activities, insurance, real estate financial activities, nonfinancial businesses, owning voting shares in nonfinancial firms, and foreign and domestic bank restrictions to enter the domestic banking market	BRSS
Banks' assets (% of GDP)	Total assets held by deposit money banks as a % of GDP	GFDD
Macro controls		
GDP per capita growth (mean, five years)	Mean of five-year (including the current) annual percentage growth rate of GDP per capita, based on constant local currency	WDI
Log (population)	Natural logarithm of the total population in a country	WDI
Inflation, consumer prices (annual %)	Inflation, consumer prices (annual %)	WDI
Enablers of digital payments		
School enrollment, secondary (% gross)	Ratio of total enrollment, regardless of age, to the population of the age group that officially corresponds to the level of education shown	WDI
Access to electricity (% of population)	% of population with access to electricity	WDI
Individuals using the internet (% of population)	% of individuals who have used the internet (from any location) in the last three months	WDI
Mobile cellular subscriptions (per 100 people)	Subscriptions to a public mobile telephone service that provide access to the public switched telephone network using cellular technology	WDI

Sources: World Bank staff Robert Cull, Daniel Lederman, and Davide Mare using information from the Bank Regulation and Supervision Survey (BRSS), Global Findex database, Global Financial Development Database (GFDD), and World Development Indicators (WDI) database. See World Bank 2017, 2019a, 2019b, 2021.

Note

1. In all of the specifications in table A.1, the same number of observations is imposed to ensure that the results are not influenced by the introduction of different countries in the estimations. The same specifications were run, and the number of countries included in the estimations was maximized—that is, countries were only dropped if the whole set of variables was not available in each specification.

References

World Bank. 2017. 2017 Global Financial Inclusion (Findex) (database). Washington, DC: World Bank. https://globalfindex .worldbank.org.

World Bank. 2019a. Bank Regulation and Supervision Survey (database). Washington, DC: World Bank. https://datacatalog .worldbank.org/dataset/bank-regulation-and -supervision-survey.

World Bank. 2019b. Global Financial Development Database. Washington, DC: World Bank. http://datacatalog.worldbank .org/dataset/global-financial-development.

World Bank. 2021. World Development Indicators (database). Washington, DC: World Bank. https://datacatalog.worldbank .org/dataset/world-development-indicators.

Appendix B: Benchmark Regressions: Graphs and Statistics

This appendix presents benchmark regressions showing that the Middle East and North Africa does well or average in most indicators of coverage of information and communication technology (ICT) infrastructure services (figure B.1), particularly mobile broadband. The region overperforms with regard to the adoption of digital tools for social media purposes (figure B.2), yet underperforms with regard to the adoption of digital tools for economic purposes—digital payments (figure B.3) and financial accounts (figure B.4)—as well as the quality of ICT services such as download speeds (figure B.5), while the region's internet prices are on par with those of other countries (in addition to being below the 2 percent affordability threshold established by the International Telecommunication Union) (figure B.6).

The Middle East and North Africa's underperformance on digital payment indicators suggests issues related to lack of competition in both the finance sector and ICT services as well as to ICT infrastructure provision being dominated by state-owned enterprises.

This appendix also presents statistical tables comprising key ICT indicators for each Middle East and North African country and regional averages, grouped by ICT service coverage (table B.1), adoption of digital technologies, notably digital finance (table B.2) and enterprise use (table B.3); and ICT enablers, notably e-governance (table B.4) and quality of institutions (table B.5).

ICT Coverage—Correlations of ICT Infrastructure with GDP per Capita

FIGURE B.1   Coverage of Information and Communication Technology Infrastructure in the Middle East and North Africa and Rest of the World, by GDP per Capita, 2019

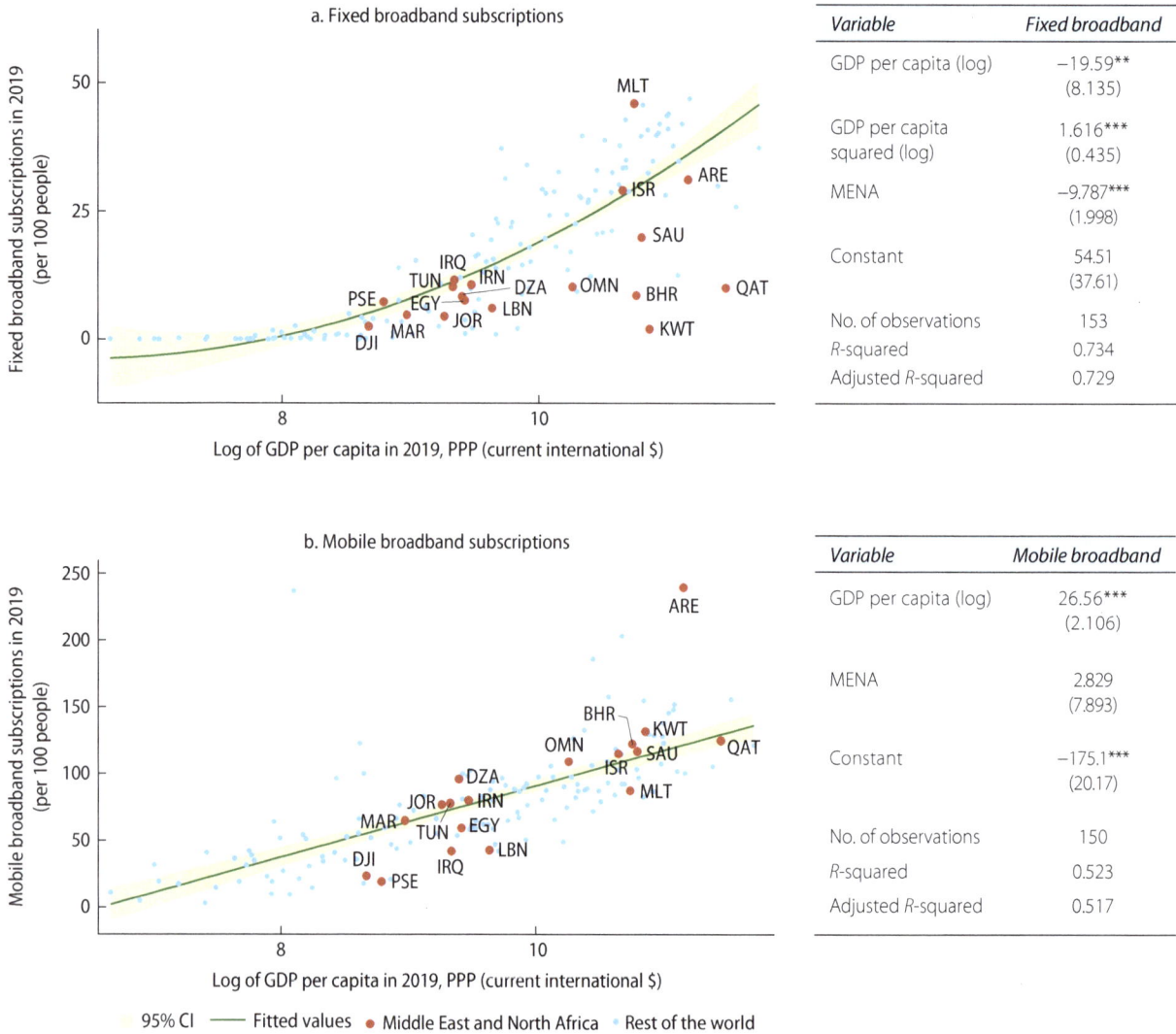

a. Fixed broadband subscriptions

Variable	Fixed broadband
GDP per capita (log)	−19.59**
	(8.135)
GDP per capita squared (log)	1.616***
	(0.435)
MENA	−9.787***
	(1.998)
Constant	54.51
	(37.61)
No. of observations	153
R-squared	0.734
Adjusted R-squared	0.729

b. Mobile broadband subscriptions

Variable	Mobile broadband
GDP per capita (log)	26.56***
	(2.106)
MENA	2.829
	(7.893)
Constant	−175.1***
	(20.17)
No. of observations	150
R-squared	0.523
Adjusted R-squared	0.517

95% CI   —— Fitted values   ● Middle East and North Africa   · Rest of the world

Figure continues next page

FIGURE B.1   **Coverage of Information and Communication Technology Infrastructure in the Middle East and North Africa and Rest of the World, by GDP per Capita, 2019 (*continued*)**

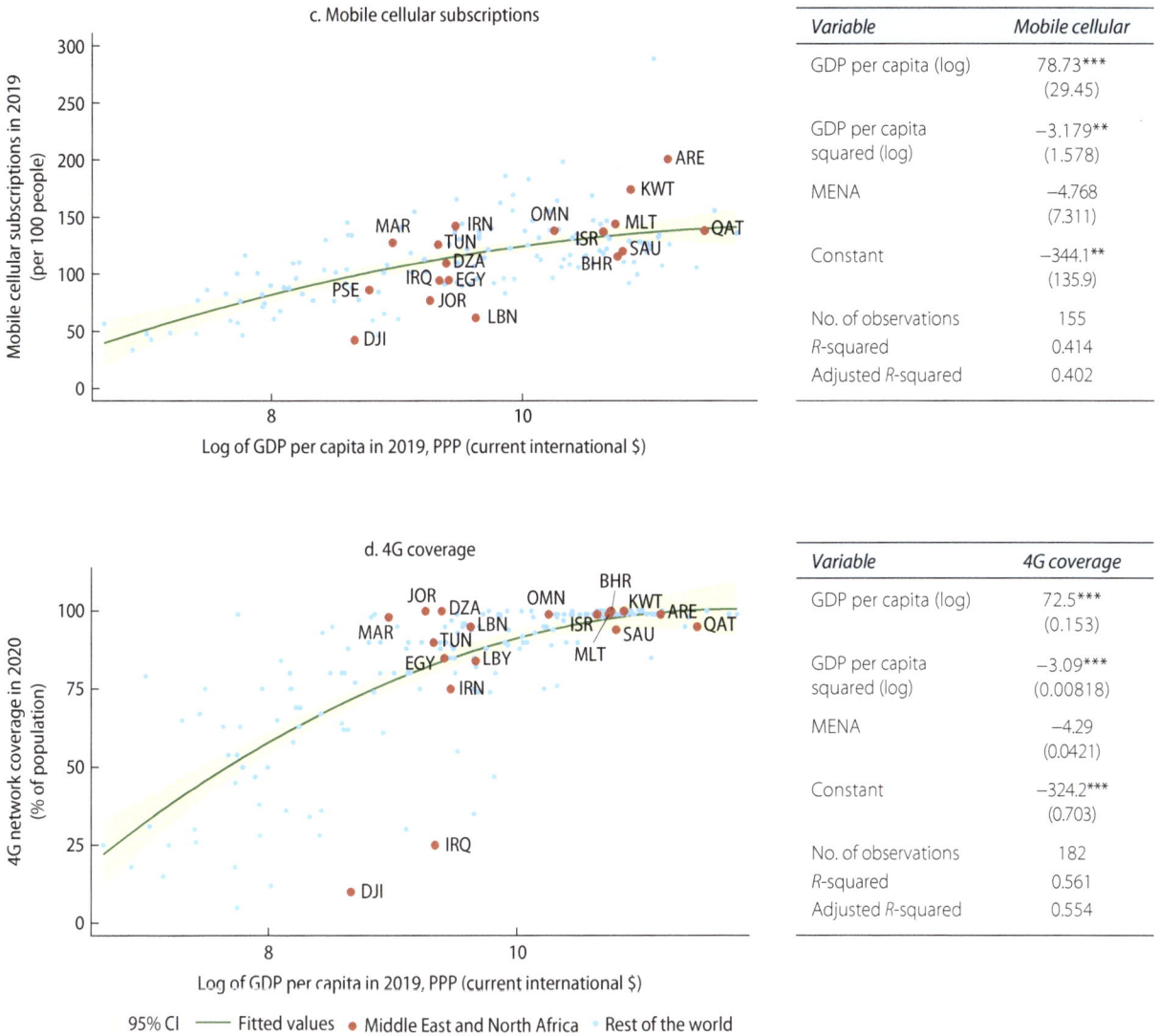

c. Mobile cellular subscriptions

Variable	Mobile cellular
GDP per capita (log)	78.73***
	(29.45)
GDP per capita squared (log)	−3.179**
	(1.578)
MENA	−4.768
	(7.311)
Constant	−344.1**
	(135.9)
No. of observations	155
R-squared	0.414
Adjusted R-squared	0.402

d. 4G coverage

Variable	4G coverage
GDP per capita (log)	72.5***
	(0.153)
GDP per capita squared (log)	−3.09***
	(0.00818)
MENA	−4.29
	(0.0421)
Constant	−324.2***
	(0.703)
No. of observations	182
R-squared	0.561
Adjusted R-squared	0.554

95% CI   —— Fitted values   ● Middle East and North Africa   · Rest of the world

Source: Original figures for this publication.
Note: CI = confidence interval. MENA = Middle East and North Africa. PPP = purchasing power parity.
** *p* < 0.05   *** *p* < 0.01

ICT Adoption—Digital Paradox Regressions: Correlations of Internet and Digital Payments with GDP per Capita

FIGURE B.2   **Facebook and Internet Use in the Middle East and North Africa and Rest of the World, by GDP per Capita**

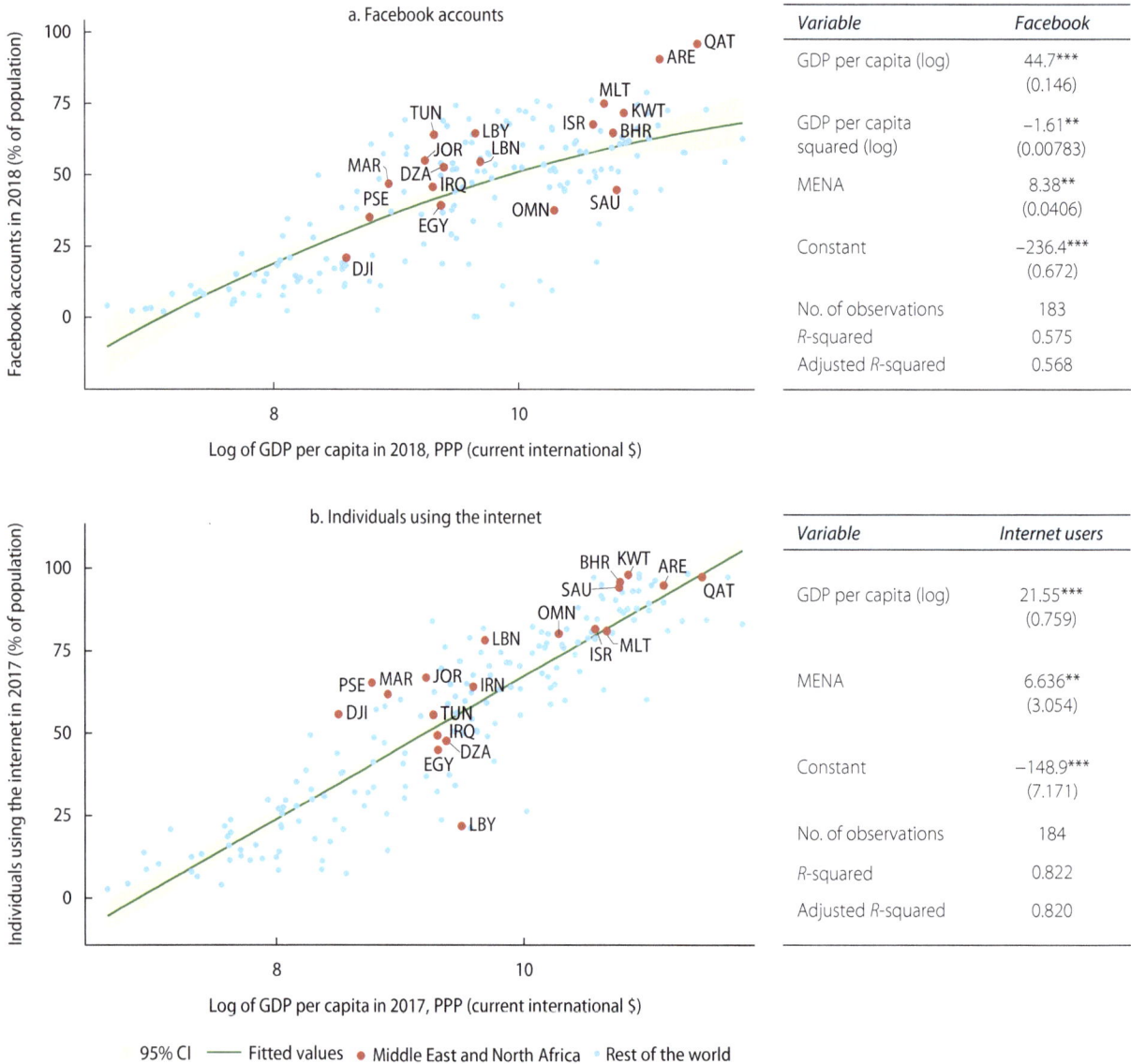

a. Facebook accounts

Variable	Facebook
GDP per capita (log)	44.7***
	(0.146)
GDP per capita squared (log)	−1.61**
	(0.00783)
MENA	8.38**
	(0.0406)
Constant	−236.4***
	(0.672)
No. of observations	183
R-squared	0.575
Adjusted R-squared	0.568

b. Individuals using the internet

Variable	Internet users
GDP per capita (log)	21.55***
	(0.759)
MENA	6.636**
	(3.054)
Constant	−148.9***
	(7.171)
No. of observations	184
R-squared	0.822
Adjusted R-squared	0.820

95% CI — Fitted values ● Middle East and North Africa ● Rest of the world

Source: Original figures for this publication.
Note: CI = confidence interval. MENA = Middle East and North Africa. PPP = purchasing power parity.
**p < 0.05   ***p < 0.01

FIGURE B.3   **Digital Payments and Online Purchases in the Middle East and North Africa and Rest of the World, by GDP per Capita**

a. Digital payments

Variable	Digital payments
GDP per capita (log)	−72.74***
	(16.05)
GDP per capita squared (log)	5.034***
	(0.869)
MENA	−15.32***
	(4.050)
Constant	287.1***
	(73.21)
No. of observations	141
R-squared	0.752
Adjusted R-squared	0.746

Log of GDP per capita in 2017, PPP (current international $)

b. Online purchases

Variable	Made online purchase
GDP per capita (log)	−96.44***
	(12.02)
GDP per capita squared (log)	6.067***
	(0.651)
MENA	−8.430***
	(3.032)
Constant	383.4***
	(54.80)
No. of observations	141
R-squared	0.780
Adjusted R-squared	0.775

Log of GDP per capita in 2017, PPP (current international $)

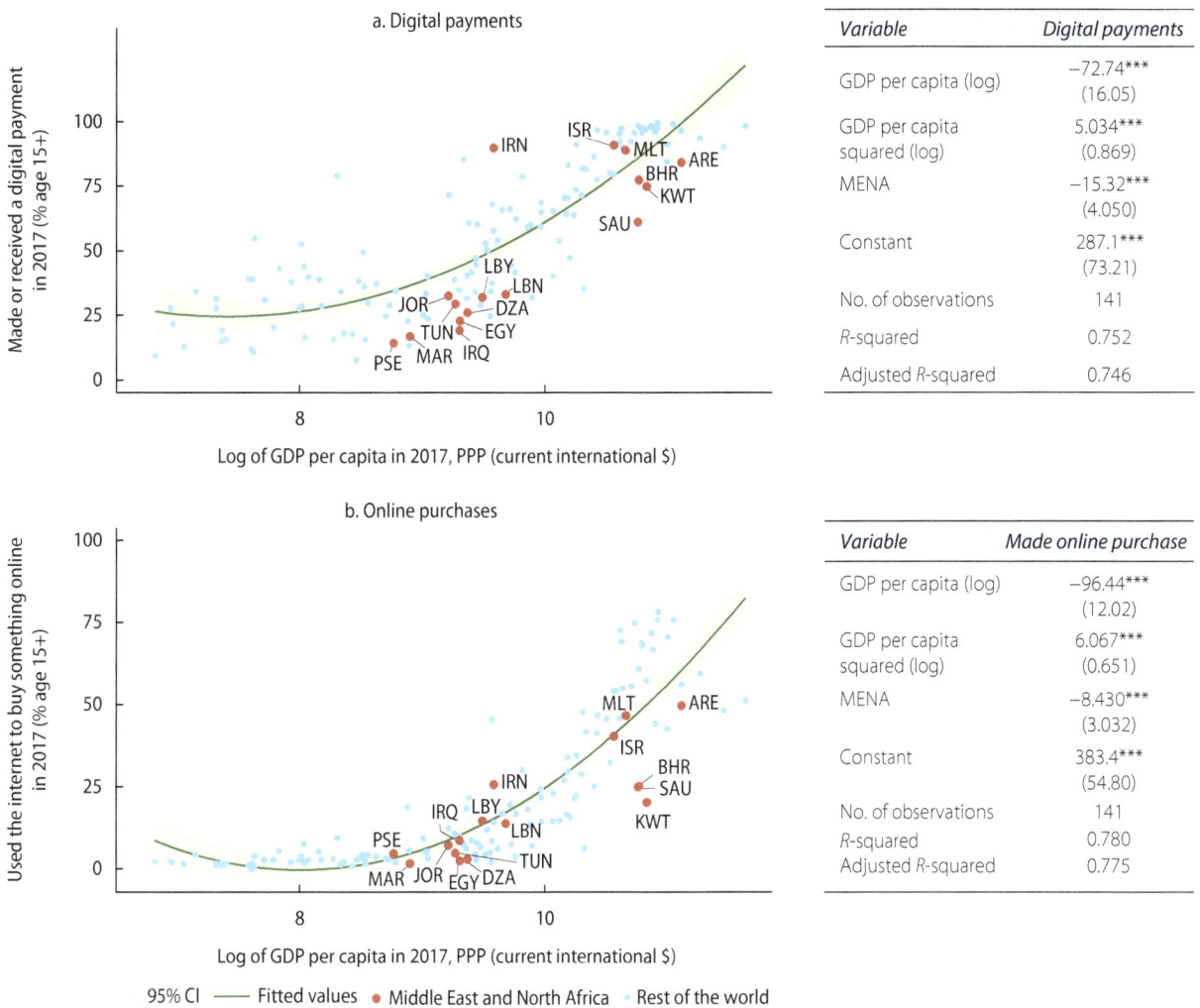

95% CI   —— Fitted values   ● Middle East and North Africa   · Rest of the world

Source: Original figures for this publication.
Note: The Findex variable for digital payments is "made or received digital payments in the past year (% age 15+)." This indicator captures the percentage of respondents who report using mobile money, a debit or credit card, or a mobile phone to make a payment from an account or who report using the internet to pay bills or to buy something online in the past 12 months. The Findex variable for online payments is "used the internet to buy something online in the past year (% age 15+)," which includes respondents who report paying bills, sending or receiving remittances, receiving payments for agricultural products, receiving government transfers, receiving wages, or receiving a public sector pension directly from or into a financial institution account or through a mobile money account in the past 12 months. This indicator is a subset of the digital payments indicator. CI = confidence interval. MENA = Middle East and North Africa. PPP = purchasing power parity.
**p < 0.05   ***p < 0.01

ICT Adoption—Correlations of Financial and Mobile Money Accounts with GDP per Capita

FIGURE B.4   **Use of Financial Accounts in the Middle East and North Africa and Rest of the World, by GDP per Capita, 2017**

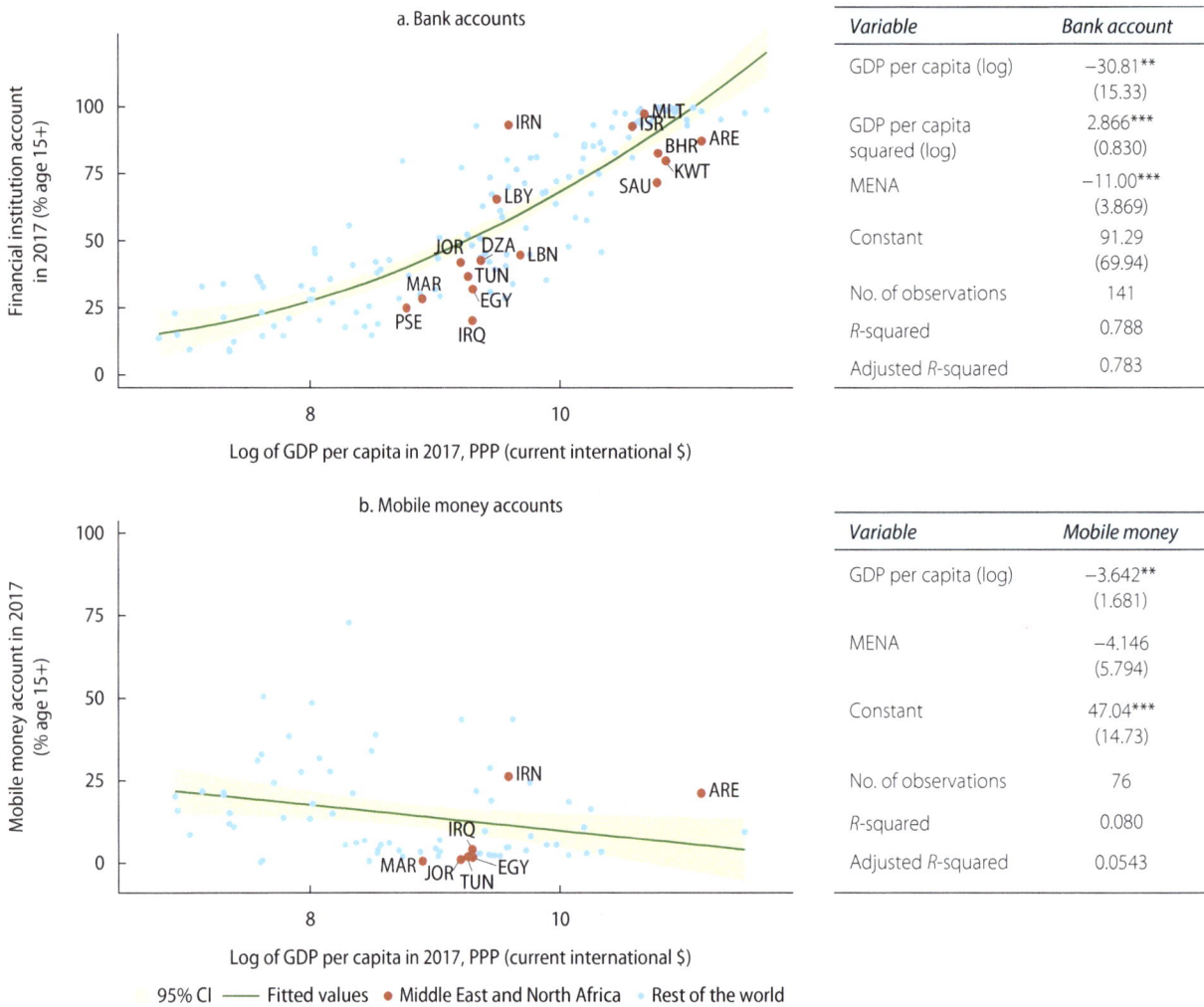

a. Bank accounts

Variable	Bank account
GDP per capita (log)	−30.81**
	(15.33)
GDP per capita squared (log)	2.866***
	(0.830)
MENA	−11.00***
	(3.869)
Constant	91.29
	(69.94)
No. of observations	141
R-squared	0.788
Adjusted R-squared	0.783

b. Mobile money accounts

Variable	Mobile money
GDP per capita (log)	−3.642**
	(1.681)
MENA	−4.146
	(5.794)
Constant	47.04***
	(14.73)
No. of observations	76
R-squared	0.080
Adjusted R-squared	0.0543

95% CI   —— Fitted values   ● Middle East and North Africa   · Rest of the world

Source: Original figures for this publication.
Note: CI = confidence interval. MENA = Middle East and North Africa. PPP = purchasing power parity.
** *p* < 0.05   *** *p* < 0.01

ICT Quality Indicators—Correlations of Download Speeds and Price Correlations with GDP per Capita

FIGURE B.5   **Download Speeds in the Middle East and North Africa and Rest of the World, by GDP per Capita, 2019**

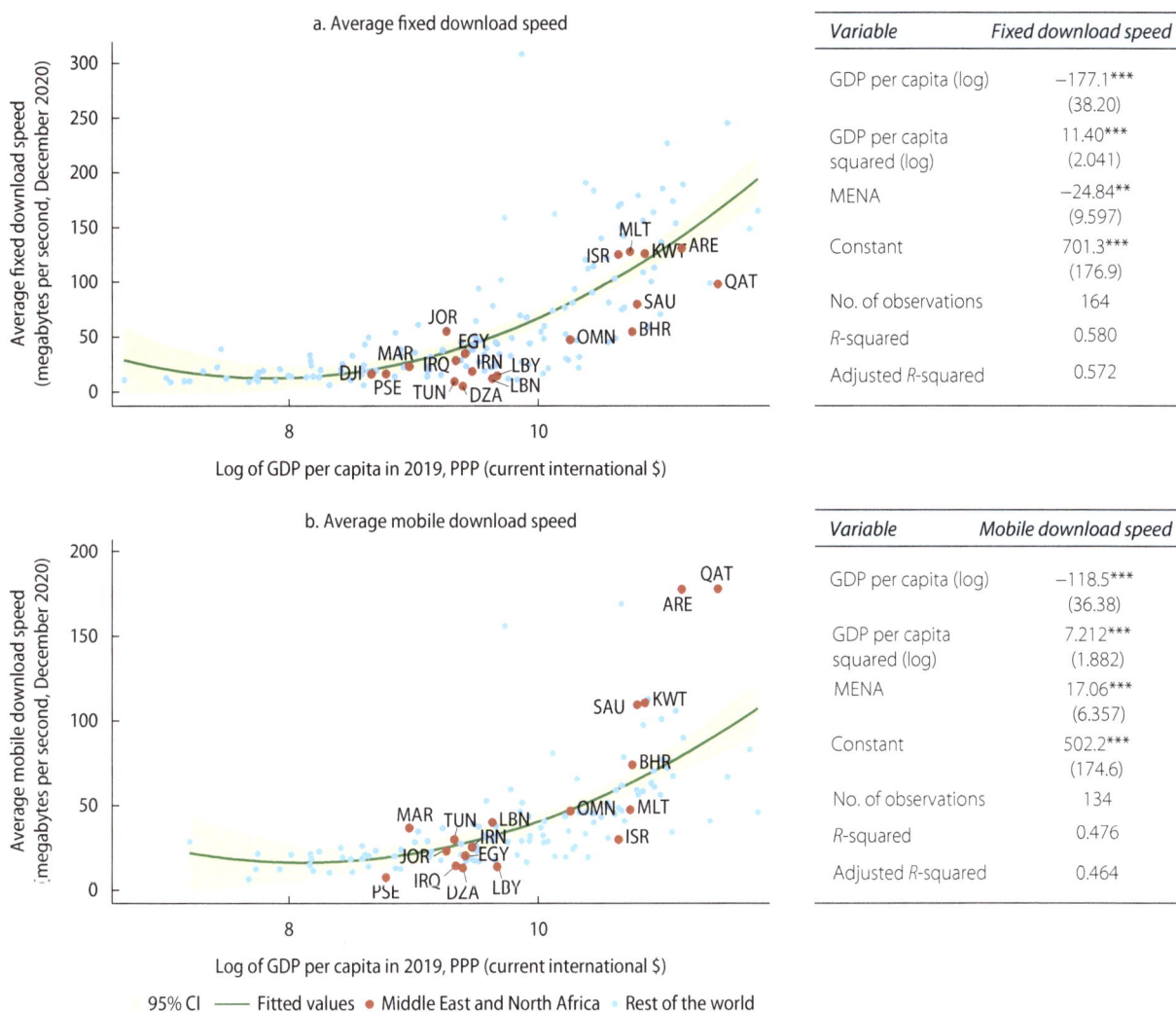

a. Average fixed download speed

Variable	Fixed download speed
GDP per capita (log)	−177.1***
	(38.20)
GDP per capita squared (log)	11.40***
	(2.041)
MENA	−24.84**
	(9.597)
Constant	701.3***
	(176.9)
No. of observations	164
R-squared	0.580
Adjusted R-squared	0.572

b. Average mobile download speed

Variable	Mobile download speed
GDP per capita (log)	−118.5***
	(36.38)
GDP per capita squared (log)	7.212***
	(1.882)
MENA	17.06***
	(6.357)
Constant	502.2***
	(174.6)
No. of observations	134
R-squared	0.476
Adjusted R-squared	0.464

95% CI ——— Fitted values ● Middle East and North Africa ● Rest of the world

Source: Original figures for this publication.
Note: CI = confidence interval. MENA = Middle East and North Africa. PPP = purchasing power parity.
** $p < 0.05$ *** $p < 0.01$

FIGURE B.6   User Prices of Data in the Middle East and North Africa and Rest of the World, by GDP per Capita, 2019

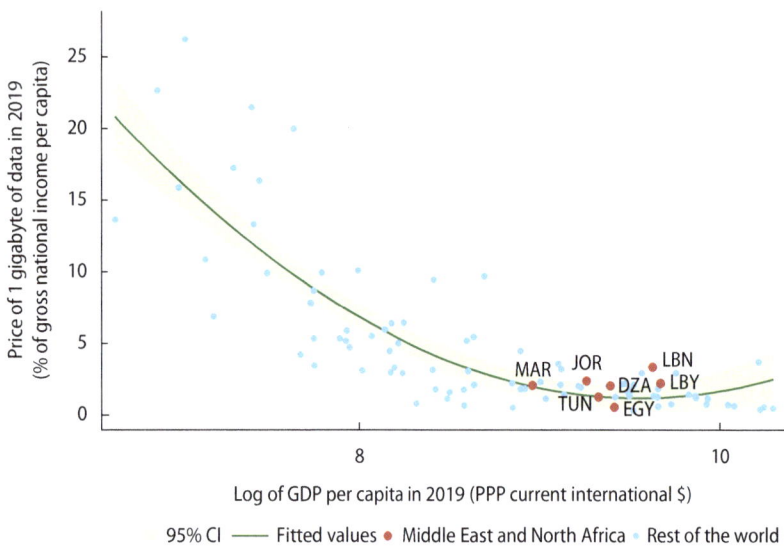

Variable	Price of 1 gigabyte of data
GDP per capita (log)	−45.6***
	(0.0646)
GDP per capita squared (log)	2.39***
	(0.00374)
MENA	0.711
	(0.0120)
Constant	218.7***
	(0.277)
No. of observations	94
R-squared	0.697
Adjusted R-squared	0.687

Source: Original figure for this publication.
Note: CI = confidence interval. MENA = Middle East and North Africa. PPP = purchasing power parity.
*** $p < 0.01$

Digital Economy: Selected Statistical Indicators

TABLE B.1 **ICT Infrastructure Coverage**

Economy or region	% of individuals using the internet	Fixed broadband connections per 100 inhabitants	Active mobile broadband subscriptions per 100 inhabitants	% of population with 4G coverage	Telecom Infrastructure Index
Economy					
Algeria	48	8.3	96.0	100	58
Bahrain	96	8.6	122.6	100	83
Djibouti	56	2.5	23.6	10	25
Egypt, Arab Rep.	45	7.6	59.3	85	47
Iran, Islamic Rep.	64	10.6	80.2	75	62
Iraq	49	11.6	42.1	25	54
Israel	82	29.1	115.0	99	87
Jordan	67	4.5	77.0	100	55
Kuwait	98	2.0	131.8	100	79
Lebanon	78	6.1	42.8	95	41
Libya	22	—	—	84	35
Malta	81	46.0	87.2	99	92
Morocco	62	4.8	64.9	98	58
Oman	80	10.2	109.1	99	70
Qatar	97	10.1	124.8	95	82
Saudi Arabia	94	19.8	116.9	94	84
Syrian Arab Republic	34	8.7	11.5	88	38
Tunisia	56	10.2	77.8	90	64
United Arab Emirates	95	31.2	239.9	99	93
West Bank and Gaza	65	7.3	19.3	—	—
Yemen, Rep.	27	—	—	—	18
Region					
East Asia and Pacific	54	14.8	105.2	83	51
Europe and Central Asia	76	31.0	97.4	95	77
Latin America and the Caribbean	61	15.0	64.8	85	56
Middle East and North Africa	66	12.6	86.4	86	61
Excluding Gulf Cooperation Council, Malta, and Israel	*52*	*7.5*	*54.1*	*77*	*46*
Gulf Cooperation Council	*93*	*13.7*	*140.8*	*98*	*82*
North America	93	37.8	117.4	98	85
South Asia	30	3.7	52.8	85	41
Sub-Saharan Africa	22	2.1	43.1	55	30
World	55	16.7	77.7	81	55

Sources: For percentage of individuals using the internet, fixed broadband connections, and active mobile broadband subscriptions, ITU. For percentage of population with 4G coverage, GSMA Intelligence © GSMA Intelligence 2018. For Telecom Infrastructure Index, United Nations data.
Note: For the share of individuals using the internet, data are for 2017. For fixed and mobile broadband indicators, data are for 2019. For 4G coverage, data are for 2020. For telecom Infrastructure Index, data are for 2020. All regional averages are simple averages using the latest available data. ICT = information and communication technology. — = not available.

TABLE B.2   ICT Adoption—Digital Finance
% of respondents

Economy or region	Used digital payments (% age 15+)	Used internet to buy something online (% age 15+)	Had a mobile money account (% age 15+)	Used online banking (% age 15+)	Received wages into account (% of wage recipients)
Economy					
Algeria	26	2.8	—	2	46
Bahrain	77	25	—	29	75
Djibouti	—	—	—	—	—
Egypt, Arab. Rep.	23	2.4	2	2	34
Iran, Islamic Rep.	90	25.7	26	45	84
Iraq	19	8.6	4	6	16
Israel	91	40.2	—	47	97
Jordan	33	7.1	1	4	44
Kuwait	75	20.2	—	24	82
Lebanon	33	13.8	—	5	46
Libya	32	14.6	—	8	43
Malta	89	46.6	—	43	85
Morocco	17	1.6	1	1	36
Oman	—	—	—	—	—
Qatar	—	—	—	—	—
Saudi Arabia	61	24.9	—	26	68
Syrian Arab Republic	—	—	—	—	—
Tunisia	29	4.7	2	4	56
United Arab Emirates	84	49.6	21	47	91
West Bank and Gaza	14	4.6	—	2	30
Yemen, Rep.	—	—	—	—	—
Region					
East Asia and Pacific	61	31.8	8	31	60
Europe and Central Asia	73	34.7	6	34	82
Latin America and the Caribbean	43	9.4	7	12	51
Middle East and North Africa	50	18.3	8	19	58
Excluding Gulf Cooperation Council, Malta, and Israel	*32*	*8.6*	*6*	*8*	*43*
Gulf Cooperation Council	*74*	*29.9*	*21*	*31*	*79*
North America	94	69.5	—	68	84
South Asia	26	1.6	7	8	29
Sub-Saharan Africa	35	3.6	24	23	42
World	54	20.6	15	26	60

Source: Findex database (World Bank 2017).
Note: The data for all the indicators are for 2017. All regional averages are simple averages with the latest available data. ICT = information and communication technology.
— = not available

TABLE B.3 ICT Adoption—Enterprises and E-commerce

Economy or region	Firms using email (all sectors) (%)	Firms with their own website (all sectors) (%)	B2C E-commerce Index	ICT Adoption Index
Economy				
Algeria	—	—	38	47
Bahrain	—	—	61	67
Djibouti	72	41	29	—
Egypt, Arab Rep.	56	42	39	41
Iran, Islamic Rep.	—	—	77	48
Iraq	21	15	25	—
Israel	99	67	86	67
Jordan	61	77	49	52
Kuwait	—	—	69	57
Lebanon	82	63	59	57
Libya	—	—	37	—
Malta	—	83	76	72
Morocco	97	55	43	44
Oman	—	—	68	57
Qatar	—	—	74	82
Saudi Arabia	—	—	73	60
Syrian Arab Republic	—	—	22	—
Tunisia	94	56	58	45
United Arab Emirates	—	—	84	84
West Bank and Gaza	46	30	—	—
Yemen, Rep.	22	21	19	18
Region				
East Asia and Pacific	66	34	68	67
Europe and Central Asia	85	63	78	66
Latin America and the Caribbean	83	50	48	46
Middle East and North Africa	65	50	54	56
Excluding Gulf Cooperation Council, Israel, and Malta	*61*	*45*	*41*	*44*
Gulf Cooperation Council	—	—	*72*	*68*
North America	—	—	92	70
South Asia	55	31	38	33
Sub-Saharan Africa	57	30	29	30
World	70	44	55	52

Sources: For firms using email and having a website, World Bank Enterprise Survey data. For B2C E-commerce Index, UNCTAD data. For ICT Adoption Index, WEF 2017.

Note: All regional averages are simple averages with the latest available data. Regarding the World Bank Enterprise Survey, the latest available data used for each country. All B2C E-commerce Index data are for 2019. All ICT Adoption Index data are for 2018. B2C = business-to-consumer. ICT = information and communication technology. — = not available.

TABLE B.4   **ICT Enablers—E-Government Development Index Subindexes**

Economy or region	E-Government Development Index	Online Services Index	Human Capital Index	E-Participation Index
Economy				
Algeria	52	28	70	15
Bahrain	82	79	84	77
Djibouti	27	22	34	21
Egypt, Arab Rep.	55	57	62	51
Iran, Islamic Rep.	66	59	77	46
Iraq	44	34	44	31
Israel	84	75	89	71
Jordan	53	36	68	33
Kuwait	79	84	75	90
Lebanon	50	42	66	33
Libya	37	4	74	4
Malta	85	81	83	83
Morocco	57	52	62	51
Oman	77	85	78	83
Qatar	72	66	67	65
Saudi Arabia	80	69	86	71
Syrian Arab Republic	48	54	51	51
Tunisia	65	62	70	69
United Arab Emirates	86	90	73	94
West Bank and Gaza	—	—	—	—
Yemen, Rep.	30	32	41	31
Region				
East Asia and Pacific	59	53	72	55
Europe and Central Asia	79	74	86	76
Latin America and the Caribbean	62	56	74	57
Middle East and North Africa	61	56	68	54
Excluding Gulf Cooperation Council, Israel, and Malta	*49*	*40*	*60*	*37*
Gulf Cooperation Council	*79*	*79*	*77*	*80*
North America	89	89	91	97
South Asia	52	59	55	57
Sub-Saharan Africa	38	37	47	36
World	60	56	69	57

Source: United Nations E-Government Development Index.
Note: All indicator data are for 2020. All regional averages are simple averages with the latest available data. ICT = information and communication technology. — = not available.

TABLE B.5   **ICT Enablers—Quality of Institutions**

Economy or region	Statistical Capacity Score	Health Security Index	Cybersecurity Index	Freedom on the Net Index
Economy				
Algeria	52	24	26	—
Bahrain	—	39	59	29
Djibouti	59	23	—	—
Egypt, Arab Rep.	86	40	84	26
Iran, Islamic Rep.	79	38	64	15
Iraq	34	26	26	—
Israel	—	47	78	—
Jordan	82	42	56	47
Kuwait	—	46	60	—
Lebanon	44	43	19	52
Libya	28	26	21	49
Malta	—	37	48	—
Morocco	67	44	43	54
Oman	—	43	87	—
Qatar	—	41	86	—
Saudi Arabia	—	49	88	25
Syrian Arab Republic	27	20	—	17
Tunisia	71	34	54	64
United Arab Emirates	—	47	81	28
West Bank and Gaza	77	—	—	—
Yemen, Rep.	39	19	2	—
Region				
East Asia and Pacific	63	40	51	49
Europe and Central Asia	73	52	72	61
Latin America and the Caribbean	67	38	31	54
Middle East and North Africa	57	36	54	37
Excluding Gulf Cooperation Council, Israel, and Malta	*57*	*31*	*39*	*41*
Gulf Cooperation Council	—	*44*	*77*	*27*
North America	—	79	91	82
South Asia	68	37	39	44
Sub-Saharan Africa	59	31	29	52
World	64	40	49	52

Sources: For the Statistical Capacity Score, World Bank data. For the Health Security Index, Johns Hopkins University data. For the Cybersecurity Index, the International Telecommunication Union of the United Nations. For the Freedom on the Net Index, Freedom House.
Note: The Statistical Capacity Score is for 2019. The Health Security Index is for 2019. The Cybersecurity Index is for 2018. The Freedom on the Net Index is for 2019. ICT = information and communication technology. — = not available.

References

Freedom House. 2019. *Freedom on the Net Index*. Washington, DC: Freedom House. http://freedomhouse.org/report/freedom-net.

GSMA (Global System for Mobile Communications Association). Various years. GSMA Intelligence Database. https://www.gsmaintelligence.com /data/.

ITU (International Telecommunication Union). 2018. Global Cybersecurity Index. Version 4. Geneva: ITU. https://www.ituy.int/en/ITU-D /cybersecurity.

Johns Hopkins University. 2019. *GHS Index: Global Health Security Index; Building Collective Action and Accountability*. Baltimore, MD: Johns Hopkins University, Center for Health Security; Nuclear Threat Initiative.

UNCTAD (United Nations Conference on Trade and Development). 2019. "B2C E-commerce Index 2019." UNCTAD Technical Note on ICT Development 14, UNCTAD, Geneva.

United Nations. 2020. E-Government Development Index Knowledge Base. https:// publicadministration.un.org/egovkb.

WEF (World Economic Forum). 2017. *The Global Competitiveness Report 2017–2018*. Geneva: WEF. https://www.weforum.org/reports/the -global-competitiveness-report-2017-2018.

World Bank. 2017. Global Findex (database). Washington, DC: World Bank. https:// globalfindex.worldbank.org/.

World Bank. 2019. "Data on Statistical Capacity." World Bank, Washington, DC. https:// datacatalog.worldbank.org/dataset/data -statistical-capacity.

World Bank. Various years. World Bank Enterprise Surveys (database). https://www .enterprisesurveys.org/en/enterprisesurveys.

Appendix C: Description of New Mobile Data Technology Adoption Rankings

This appendix describes the construction of telecommunication sector indicators relating to the adoption of telecommunication technology, liberalization of the telecommunication sector, foreign participation in telecommunication operators, and independence of the regulatory authority. For further information on these indicators and their data sources, see Arezki et al. (2021, app. table 1); for information on basic descriptive statistics on the indicators, see Arezki et al. (2021, app. table 2).

Technology Adoption Indicator

Arezki et al. (2021) construct an index of the *pace of technology adoption* by ranking each country on how quickly it adopts each telecommunication technology standard (1G through 5G). This is a balanced data set of rankings for 198 countries for 40 years since 1980, based on Telegeography's Spectrum Launched Timeline, which lists the date at which each country has adopted a given standard. Regional indexes are derived as simple averages of the countries in the region. Figure C.1, which is also featured in chapter 7, shows the evolution of the ranking for the Middle East and North Africa and for

Sub-Saharan Africa. In contrast with North America, which jumped quickly to top rank and stayed there, some regions have progressed up the technology ladder much more slowly, and others have had swings in trajectory, like the Middle East and North Africa, which has declined in ranking since 2008. Sub-Saharan Africa's ranking declined through 2006 but has since been improving (figure C.1).

The indicators were constructed to reflect the relative speed or delay in technology adoption, as follows. At each point in time, countries were grouped based on the latest standard they have adopted. Group 1 includes countries that have adopted the most advanced standard. Group 2 includes countries that have adopted the second-newest standard available to date, and so on for the other groups. Within each group, countries are ranked in the order they have adopted a given standard. Consider n countries at period t, of which x countries have launched 4G, while y countries have launched 3G. Then in this period, the x countries that have adopted 4G will rank from number 1 to x, with the country that first launched 4G being ranked first. The set of y countries only using 3G will rank from

FIGURE C.1 **Mobile Technology Adoption Rankings in the Middle East and North Africa and in Sub-Saharan Africa, 1981–2019**

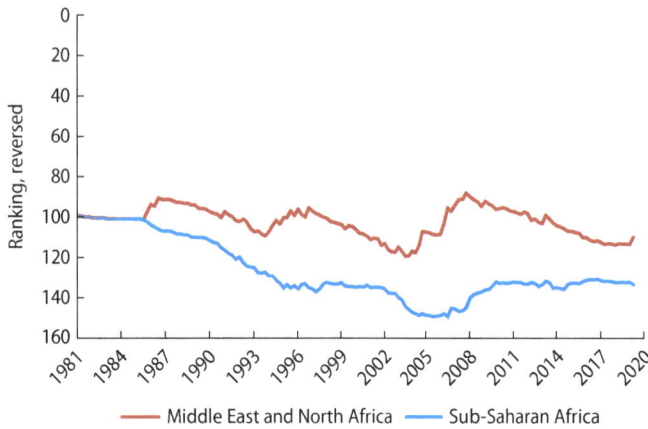

Source: Arezki et al. 2021.
Note: Country groups are represented by simple average rankings from all member countries for each specific year. For more details on technology adoption ranking, see Arezki et al. (2021).

x+1 to x+y, with the country that first adopted 3G ranking number x+1. If in the next period, t+1, a new generation of technologies becomes available, say 5G, the frontier of technology will shift. In period t+1, the country that first adopts 5G now ranks first, and all other countries' earlier rankings go down by one notch if they do not adopt the 5G standard. As more countries catch up and adopt 5G, countries not adopting new standards will fall further in the ranking, indicating the delay in technology adoption. However, the indicator is such that, after a given country adopts the latest technology standard and before another new standard becomes available, that country's ranking will not be affected by other countries adopting the same technology afterward.

Considering 1G to 5G telecommunication standards, the indicator shows increasing speeds of adoption from 1G to 5G. For example, it took 14 years for the group of 1G adopters to reach 50 countries, 10 years for the group of 2G adopters to reach 100 countries, and only 6 years for the group of 4G adopters to reach more than 100 countries. The standards that cover most countries and years (the largest area in Arezki et al. 2021, fig. 2) are 2G and 4G.

Indicator of Telecommunication Regulatory Authority Independence

Independence of the telecommunication regulatory authority is captured by data from the International Telecommunication Union (ITU) regulatory trackers, which cover 180 countries from 2003 to 2017. The indicator is based on the sum of the score of the answers to 10 related questions in cluster 1 of the ITU data set. Each answer has a full score of 2, such as having a separate telecommunication or information and communication technology (ICT) regulator, autonomy in decision making, accountability, and others. A higher score indicates a more independent regulatory authority. In the analysis, the indicator is normalized between 0 and 1 for simplicity. Figure C.2, which is also featured in chapter 7, shows that the Middle East and North Africa has less regulatory independence than other middle-income countries and Sub-Saharan Africa.

Liberalization and Foreign Participation Indexes

Liberalization of the telecommunication sector is defined as the time when competition was instigated in the market, constructed using data from Telegeography on the month and year in which the telecommunication industry was liberalized in each country. The liberalization variable reflects the date of promulgation of legislation allowing the entry of new operators offering services in competition with the incumbents. When countries have liberalized in stages—for example, local telephony, domestic long distance, and international long distance—the date of international liberalization is used as the actual date of liberalization. (The data set is available for more than 200 economies, and the earliest liberalization is as early as 1984.[1])

As the liberalization variable reflects statutory (de jure) liberalization, another variable—foreign participation in the telecommunication sector—is also constructed to capture the effective (de facto) liberalization of the sector. This new indicator combines the market share database and groups-ownership database from GSMA Intelligence. The market share database provides the market share of each telecommunication operator, and the group's ownership database provides each operator's ownership structure.[2]

Foreign Participation Rate (de facto liberalization)

A country's level of foreign participation in the telecommunication sector depends on market size, on the degree of dominance and competitiveness of the main domestic operator, and on the country's liberalization trajectory. To construct the indicator, first, a group owner is defined as being international for each time period, if the owner operates in multiple countries.[3] Then, the rate of foreign participation for country c at time t is calculated as follows:

$$f_{c,t} = \sum_{p \in P_{c,t}} \left(s_{p,c,t} \times \sum_{w \in W_{p,t}} n_{w,p,c,t} \right), \qquad (C.1)$$

where $P_{c,t}$ comprises all operators that have a positive market share in country c at time t, $W_{p,t}$ comprises all international owners of operator p at time t, $s_{p,c,t}$ is the market share of operator p in country c at time t, and $n_{w,p,c,t}$ is ownership share of operator p by owner w.

For example, consider a given country with two telecommunication operators, A and B, with market shares of s_A and s_B, respectively. Domestic owner D_A owns d_A percent of operator A, international owner I_{A1} owns i_{A1} percent, and international owner I_{A2} owns i_{A2} percent. Domestic owner D_{B1} owns d_{B1} percent of operator B, domestic owner D_{B2} owns d_{B2} percent, and international owner I_B owns i_B percent. Then the foreign participation rate in this country is equal to $s_A \times (i_{A1} + i_{A2}) + s_B \times i_B$.

Regions where domestic telecommunication operators are dominant in their local markets yet have a global reach because of their competitiveness, have lower shares of foreign participation (notably, Australia, East Asia, North America, and Western Europe). Other countries with low shares of foreign

FIGURE C.2   ICT Regulatory Authority Independence Index in the Middle East and North Africa and in Sub-Saharan Africa and by Country Income Group, 2017

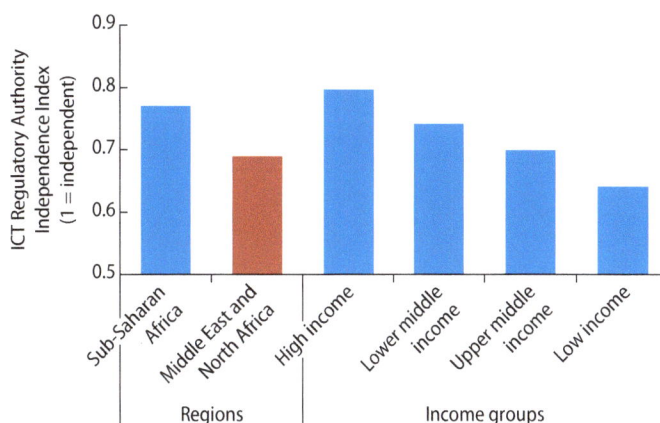

Source: Arezki et al. 2021, based on International Telecommunication Union data and World Bank calculations.
Note: Bars represent independence of the ICT regulatory authority. Scores are normalized to range between 0 and 1. Country groups are represented by the simple average of all member countries. ICT = information and communication technology.

FIGURE C.3   Share of Liberalized Countries in the Middle East and North Africa and in Sub-Saharan Africa, 2000–18

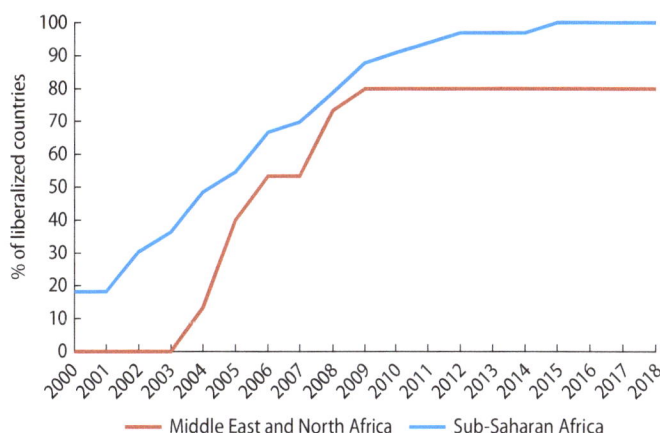

Source: World Bank staff calculations based on Telegeography data.
Note: Lines display the share of countries that have liberalized information and communication technology. For more details on telecommunication liberalization, see Arezki et al. (2021).

participation are countries that have limited effective liberalization, because state-owned enterprises dominate their local markets yet lack a global reach as they are not competitive. Developing regions, in general, have higher foreign participation in their telecommunication sector, due to progressive liberalization since the 1990s. Figure C.3, which is also featured in chapter 7, shows

FIGURE C.4 **Share of Foreign Participation in the Middle East and North Africa and in Sub-Saharan Africa, 2000–18**

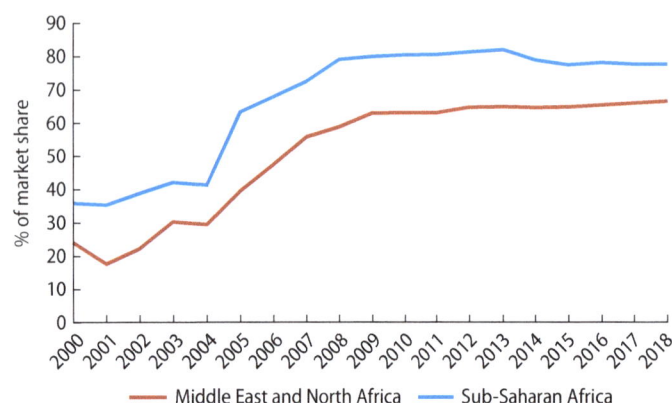

Source: Arezki et al. 2021.
Note: Regions are represented by the simple average of the foreign participation rate in their member countries. For more details on the foreign participation rate, see Arezki et al. (2021).

the increasing liberalization of the telecommunication sectors in the Middle East and North Africa and in Sub-Saharan Africa, while figure C.4 (also featured in chapter 7) shows the corresponding upward trends in foreign participation in the sector since 2000 to levels among the highest in the world.

Notes

1. Isle of Man, Japan, United Kingdom, and United States.
2. When ownership data are not available, the operator's ownership structure, including whether the owner is domestic or international, was used. Only trustworthy sources, including Telegeography, the Stock Exchange Commission, Internet Society, and interviews of telecommunication experts, were used.
3. For each owner, all countries are identified for which the group owner holds more than 5 percent of voting rights of its operators. If in a given period, more than one country is listed in the group owner's operations, then the owner is considered "international" in that period.

Reference

Arezki, Rabah, Vianney Dequiedt, Rachel Yuting Fan, and Carlo Maria Rossotto. 2021. "Liberalization, Technology Adoption, and Stock Returns: Evidence from Telecom." Policy Research Working Paper 9561, World Bank, Washington, DC. https://openknowledge .worldbank.org/handle/10986/35210.

www.ingramcontent.com/pod-product-compliance
Lightning Source LLC
Chambersburg PA
CBHW041722210326
41598CB00007B/746